CONTENTS

Delicious Mango Bread
Olive Feta Bread
Apple Zucchini Bread
Herb Cheddar Cheese Bread
Bacon Jalapeno Pepper Bread
Easy No Yeast Bread
Herb Bread
Whole Wheat Bread
Easy Sandwich Bread
Cinnamon Carrot Bread
Nut Orange Bread
Mixed Nut Strawberry Bread
Spelt Bread
Nut & Seed Bread
 BREADSTICKS

Delicious Breadsticks
Italian Breadsticks
Cheese Garlic Breadsticks
Easy Cheesy Breadsticks
Fluffy Breadsticks
Soft & Flavorful Breadsticks
Keto Breadsticks
Oregano Breadsticks
Zucchini Breadsticks
Keto Garlic Cheese Breadsticks
Cinnamon Breadsticks
Italian Breadsticks
Taco Chicken Breadsticks
Easy Pizza Dough Breadsticks
Delicious Zucchini Breadsticks
Easy Pesto Breadsticks
Rosemary Cheese Breadsticks
Cauliflower Breadsticks
Tasty Italian Breadsticks

Cheesiest Breadsticks

Broccoli Breadsticks

Perfect Sour Cream Breadsticks

Garlic Almond Flour Breadsticks

Sesame Seed Breadsticks

Almond Coconut Flour Breadsticks

Simple Puff Pastry Breadsticks

Cranberry Breadsticks

Buttery Cinnamon Breadsticks

Amaranth Breadsticks

Broccoli Cheese Breadsticks

BUNS

Whole Wheat Buns

Perfect Hamburger Buns

Tasty Hamburger Buns

Soft Burger Buns

Fluffy Raisin Buns

Keto Buns

Almond Flour Buns

Jalapeno Wheat Buns

PRETZELS, MUFFINS, CAKES, BAGUETTE, & SNACKS

Soft Pretzels

French Baguette

Coconut Flour Baguette

Carrot Muffins

Lemon Muffins

Delicious Carrot Cake

Raspberry Muffins

Delicious Mini Chocolate Cake

Apple Cinnamon Cake

Cranberry Muffins

Simple Butter Cake

Ricotta Strawberry Cake

Cinnamon Cake

HOW I FELL IN LOVE WITH BAKING FRESH BREAD AT HOME

If you told me a few years ago I would be here writing a book about bread baking, I wouldn't believe you. I've never been much of a baker. Sure, I made batches of cookies now and then, but I never thought I'd try my hand at homemade bread. My grandmother was the baker in our family. I remember watching her and sometimes "helping" her knead the dough, but I never really thought about following in her footsteps.

When Grandma died, I started going through old photos and recipes. So many of the pictures showed her in the kitchen. Baking was her love language. I decided to make one of her favorite bread recipes to feel closer to her in my grief. It was a classic sourdough. I remember that she always used it for BLTs, cooking the bacon in the oven and bringing in tomatoes from her garden. In my memory, even the mayonnaise tasted better, though I'm sure it was just a normal jar from the store.

Let me tell you, my first few attempts at baking bread did not go very well. I'm sure many baking beginners can relate. Sourdough is not the easiest bread type to start with, which is why these days, I tell beginners to start with something simpler if they aren't ready for a challenge. I was determined to master that sourdough though, so I kept at it. I read all I could about how to take care of my starter, watching it like a hawk, and reading about the science going on in that jar. Being patient and slowing down helped a lot, too. I learned that being precise and careful results in better bread!

Now, I usually bake bread when I'm feeling down. I find the process relaxes me. Carefully weighing the ingredients, mixing them, and getting out any aggressive feelings by kneading the dough brings me back to myself. I'm not alone in this! Research shows that baking can help alleviate symptoms of depression and anxiety. I know I always feel a sense of accomplishment when I smell bread baking. Even if the rest of my day didn't go the way I wanted, I still created something. If I don't want to spend as much time getting the bread ready, I'll choose a recipe that doesn't require kneading, but I'll still feel better afterward. I love bread in all its forms, but my favorite is still the sourdough recipe my grandmother used. I have a BLT at least once a week, though I also love a thick slice, toasted, spread with salted butter and raspberry jam.

These days, I actually don't buy bread that often anymore. On a free day, I'll bake a bunch and refrigerate or freeze what I won't eat in the next few days. I love giving away my homemade bread, too, especially around the holidays or when someone is going through hard times. Food is love. I hope this book helps you express your love to your friends and family.

Warm regards,

Christine

INTRODUCTION

There's something special about homemade bread. Everyone should experience the satisfaction that comes from kneading dough, letting it rise, and waiting patiently while the fragrance wafts from the oven. In the past, everyone made their own bread. Based on archaeological research, humans have been baking bread for thousands of years. In more recent years, bread-making became more industrialized. Now, there's more variety and better quality store-bought bread to choose from. Still, baking bread at home can't be denied.

In this book, you'll be introduced to bread-baking and all the great recipes you can make. The introduction includes a brief history of bread, why you should bake your own, and the different types of bread out there. I'll also list the must-have ingredients and tools that will make the process as smooth as possible. A little worried about baking bread for the first time? You can find tips for success and solutions to the most common problems.

Whether you want to try your hand at classic loaves, breadsticks, buns, pretzels, or quick bread like muffins, cakes, and snacks, you'll find what you're looking for in this book. Making homemade bread can relieve stress, help you save on your grocery bill, and - best of all - let you share something delicious with the people you love!

Chapter 1: A Brief History of Bread-Making

Like everything in this world, bread-making has evolved. Ancient humans didn't just start baking fluffy white loaves, tangy sourdough, or crunchy baguettes one day after feeling hungry. A lot happened to transform the watery porridge prehistoric humans ate into the bread we see today. Where did bread come from? How has it changed?

The first bread

While investigating stone fireplaces, a team of researchers discovered the charred remains of ancient bread crumbs. Upon closer inspection, they learned that the crumbs most likely came from a mixed-grain flatbread. They dated the crumbs to around 14,400 years ago. This makes the discovery the oldest evidence of bread-making.

Who made this bread? Experts believe the bakers were the Natufians, a people group that lived in the Eastern Mediterranian between 12,500 and 9,500 BCE. Based on how old the crumbs were, this means the Natufians were making bread before they set up permanent agricultural systems. For many years, we assumed humans domesticated grain before bread-making. These charred crumbs suggest otherwise.

The bread was likely made by grinding wild grains and a starchy root into a fine flour. After mixing this with water, the dough was baked on a hot, flat stone or in the hot ashes of a fire. It would have been a time-consuming process, but the Natufians' willingness to go through it suggests they found it worthwhile. They might have started domesticating grains to make bread-making easier. It sure seems like humans loved bread so much that they started an agricultural revolution - transforming human civilization - so making bread was more convenient.

The oldest bread (so far) dates back over 14,000 years. Since then, innovations like leavening, refined flour, and technology have transformed this staple food into what we love today.

The evolution of bread

The Natufians pioneered bread-making. Over the next few thousands of years, agricultural and grains spread. Trade would have facilitated this knowledge-sharing. Over 5,000 years after the Natufians first made flatbread, the Egyptians, Mesopotamians, and Harappans depended on bread. These were the largest civilizations in the ancient world. Bread powered them, allowing them to develop social classes and artisans.

These civilizations helped bread evolve from its Natufian origins. Leavening is one of the most significant advancements in bread-making. The most common leavening, yeast, is what allows bread to rise. How does this work? Yeast eats the sugar in grain, releasing CO_2 and bubbles that make bread rise. While many believe the first leavened bread came from Egypt, there is evidence that Mesopotamians were also making it. In Egypt, commercial yeast production dates back to 300 B.C.E. Egyptians also experimented with different grains as well as honey, eggs, seeds, and spices. Making bread in the shape of animals was popular and often used for special events.

Refined flour was another big innovation. For years, people ground grains by hand using rocks. The bread would have been coarse and earthy because it included the whole grain. Around 800 B.C.E, the Mesopotamians used two flat, round stones on top of each other to grind their grains. Rotated by slaves or animals, this milling process created fine, smooth flour. Further advancements improved on this basic idea. Eating bread made with finely-milled flour showed that you had a high social status. This belief spread throughout the world. In Europe during medieval times, only the richest classes could afford white loaves. The lower classes ate rye and bran bread.

Bread in the 20th century

Bread, something that seems so uncomplicated, has been a major source of controversy and social debates. Throughout the years, peoples' views on race, class, and gender affected how society saw all food, including bread. Some bread was considered "high class" while other kinds were "low class." There were also serious concerns about food safety. In the early 20th century, changes like stricter food regulations and factories led to more mass-produced foods. In 1920s America, the "perfect" white bread symbolized the modern era and how far technology had come. People also saw this bread as safe and therefore healthy. Sliced bread, which may have been invented in Chillicothe, Missouri in 1928, captured the hearts of consumers. Only the magic of technology could produce such beautiful, even, safe slices. Within two years, 90% of the bread bought in stores was sliced.

Not everyone was happy with modern bread, though. Bernarr Macfadden, a pioneer of the health and fitness culture in the US, believed in the nutritional and moral superiority of whole wheat bread. He went so far as to say that white bread was "the staff of death." For many, assigning a moral value to bread transformed manufactured white bread into a symbol of how far America had fallen in its values. While white bread may have been technically "safe" thanks to technology, what had been sacrificed in the name of safety? Making your own bread and refusing to buy the stuff from a factory became a way to stick it to the man.

A return to rustic

The aversion to store-bought white bread paved the way for the wide variety of artisanal bread you can find today. These breads are more expensive, but many are willing to pay for something that uses better ingredients, unique grains, and more traditional processes. Artisanal breads are more nutritious, too, which is a must for many shoppers. There's also the matter of flavor. Pricier breads taste better. With all these advantages, smaller-batch, artisanal bread is here to stay.

Not so long ago, factory-made, storebought white bread was considered the best bread around. Now, people have been returning to more rustic, artisanal breads and baking more bread at home!

Why you should bake your own bread

Baking bread at home has become much more common in recent years. In our lightning-fast, work-obsessed world, choosing to bake bread when you could just buy it can be a radical act. There's often a learning curve and mistakes are pretty much inevitable. Why go through all that when you could just buy bread? What are the benefits?

Homemade bread tastes better

Taste is one of the main reasons why baking bread is worth the effort. Store-bought, no matter how high-quality it is, can never truly compare to fresh bread right from the oven. Homemade sandwich bread transforms everyday meals like PB&J and BLTs, while breadsticks and buns at a gathering impress anyone who takes a bite. Homemade sweet treats like muffins and cakes - which are covered in the recipe section of this book - are also special. Bread is often seen as only a vehicle for other ingredients, but when it's homemade, bread is a star in its own right.

Artisinal breads are expensive

It's no surprise that a homemade loaf of bread is better than store-bought, but there are really tasty breads you buy now. So, why make it? These tastier, higher-quality store-bought loaves are not cheap. Depending on the bread, artisanal can cost 3 times more than a regular loaf. While it clearly takes more time to bake bread, you can save a significant amount of money.

You can experiment

Unless you're a very experienced baker, there are certain ingredient ratios you shouldn't experiment with, but you are free to add different flavorings! Herbs, spices, dried fruit, and nuts are all usually easy additions to plain recipes. Play with glazes, seasoned salts, compound butter, and more to make your homemade creations even tastier. To make homemade bread healthier, you can also try different ingredient swaps.

Baking is good for your mental health

Bread-making isn't only delicious and affordable. It's also good for mental health. In 2017, five mental health residents at a London hospital went through six 2-hour baking sessions. Each week, they were asked how they felt. They said they felt happier, relaxed, less anxious, and more creative. Other research shows that baking is beneficial to mental health because it focuses your mind, involves all your senses, and gives you a sense of achievement. During stressful times, try baking some bread! You might find it raises your spirits.

Baking homemade bread has many benefits. It tastes better than store-bought, you can experiment with different flavors, and it can improve your mental health! Baking bread is also less expensive than buying pricey artisinal loaves.

Chapter 2: What Types Of Bread Can You Make?

When you hear the word "bread," what do you picture? Maybe you think of classic sliced sandwich bread. There are so many bread types out there, all of which can be made at home with the right ingredients and equipment! In this chapter, I'll run through a wide variety of breads and what defines them.

White bread

White bread is bread made from refined wheat flour. Unlike in the old days, you don't have to mill your own flour, so making the classic, white sandwich bread is much easier. Homemade white bread will most likely be a little healthier than store-bought. It still contains less nutrients than whole wheat or whole grain.

Whole wheat bread

Whole wheat bread is made with flour that uses the (no surprise here) whole grain. This includes the bran and germ. The bread contains more protein, fiber, and vitamins. The flavor is also richer.

Multigrain

Multigrain bread is bread that uses more than one grain. Flax, oats, wheat, and barley are common. To make your own, you can buy individual grains, but a multigrain flour mix is more convenient. Many people also add seeds to this sandwich bread. This boosts its vitamin content.

Sourdough

Sourdough is one of the most popular homemade breads these days. To make sourdough, you'll need a starter. A starter is a mix of flour and water that grows yeast in about 5 days, depending on your kitchen conditions. Sourdough bread has a unique tangy, sour flavor. It's good for digestion and blood sugar.

Rye bread

If you've ever enjoyed a pastrami or corn beef sandwich, you've most likely eaten rye bread. Depending on what part of the rye berry in the flour, the bread can be light or very dark. You'll often see recipes that use a mixture of rye and wheat flour. Rye bread, which should be chewy, has a deep, earthy flavor.

Pumpernickel

Pumpernickel is a type of rye bread made from coarsely ground whole rye berries. It originated in Germany. The traditional baking method can take as long as 24 hours at a very low temperature. That gives it its distinctive dark color. Modern recipes often skip the long bake time and call for molasses, cocoa, or coffee for color.

Flatbreads

Flatbreads include naan, pita, and tortillas. They contain no leavening or very little in the case of pita and naan. Flatbreads are common in the Middle East and Latin America. Pita breads have a pocket for other ingredients or you can wrap them. You can use naan for a variety of dishes like sandwiches, pizza, or to scoop up dips.

When you're a bread-baking beginner, there's a wide variety of bread types to choose from. Some (like quick breads and flatbreads) are easier than others, while others (like sourdough and baguettes) require more technique.

Challah

This unique braided bread is made with eggs. It's a Jewish bread traditionally served on holidays and the Sabbath. The egg yolks give the bread an almost spongy, soft texture and a light color. Honey, olive oil, and raisins can be added for more flavor and sweetness.

Brioche

Brioche is a French bread that's very soft and slightly sweet. It can be used for hamburger buns and rolls. It also makes great French toast. A yeasted bread, it's full of butter and eggs, so it has a rich taste. Brioche dough can be used for sweet Easter and Christmas treats.

Baguette

Another famous French bread, long baguettes have a chewy interior. They're made from just flour, water, yeast, and salt. While the ingredients are simple, making this bread is all about the technique.

Soda bread

Traditional Irish soda bread is made from wheat flour, baking soda, salt, and buttermilk. A dense bread, it usually has a mild flavor. It's pretty bland on its own, so it should be served with butter and jam. It's also good with stews and soups. For those who want sweetness, raisins are common.

Ciabatta

An Italian bread, this bread is flat and wide. There are many variations, but it's a great sandwich bread. It's one of the most recent types of bread, as well, as it was first made in 1982. It's now a very popular bread. It has a very wet dough.

Focaccia

Another Italian bread, focaccia is yeasted, but it's pretty flat. It's baked in sheet pans at a very high temperature. Unlike ciabatta, it's very old. It most likely dates back to ancient Rome. Common toppings include olive oil, salt, and rosemary. It's usually eaten as an appetizer or snack.

Breadsticks

Crunchy and thin, breadsticks are a very unique type of bread. They most likely date back to 17th-century Italy. Today, you can find larger, soft breadsticks in America with cheese and garlic. Traditional breadsticks, however, are as thin as pencils.

Pretzels

Pretzels originate in Germany. They are made from water, malt, salt, flour, and yeast. The dough is shaped into knots before baking. Unlike the tiny, crunchy snack pretzels, homemade baked pretzels are soft and a little chewy. You can experiment with all kinds of savory and sweet toppings and glazes. Something simple like a little melted butter and coarse salt is delicious.

Quick breads

Quick breads are leavened with baking soda and baking powder instead of yeast. As their name suggests, this means it takes much less time to make them. There are two types of quick breads: dough and batter. Batter quick breads include muffins, cornbread, and banana bread. Dough quick breads include scones and biscuits. If you're brand new to bread-making, quick breads are typically very easy.

Chapter 3: Must-Have Ingredients and Equipment To Get Started

You've decided to try your hand at baking bread, so what do you need? The vast majority of bread recipes require the same basic ingredients. Always having these on hand lets you bake when the mood strikes. There is also certain equipment you'll need. This chapter runs down what you should get.

Must-have ingredients

Some baked goods require a lot of ingredients. Broken down to its essentials, bread requires very few. It's amazing what water, flour, and yeast can transform into when baked. To make really good bread, here's what you'll need:

Flour

Bread recipes use a lot of flour. It's the main ingredient. All-purpose flour is the most basic type and lets you make a variety of baked goods. Depending on the kind of bread you're making, you'll also need flours like whole-wheat, multigrain, bread flour, cornmeal, and so on. Before starting a recipe, check to see you have the right flour in your pantry. All flours should be stored in airtight containers in a cool, dry, dark area. The fridge is also a good place, especially for whole wheat and whole grain flours. You can also freeze flour where it should stay good for up to 2 years. If you notice your flour has changed color or smells different, don't use it.

Leaveners

Unless you're making flatbread, every bread recipe will need some kind of leavening. Yeasted breads like sourdough, whole wheat, and white bread need yeast. With sourdough, you'll make your own sourdough starter and collect yeast that way. For other types of yeasted breads, you can buy packets of active dry or instant yeast. What's the difference? Most recipes call for active dry. This yeast dissolves in warm water and a little bit of sugar. This process "blooms" the yeast. Instant yeast doesn't need this bloom time and is added right into the dry ingredients.

If your recipe doesn't call for yeast, you'll most likely use a combination of baking soda and baking powder. Baking soda needs to be activated with an acid and liquid. Baking powder already contains an acid, so it only needs liquid. They are not interchangeable, so always have both in your pantry.

Sweetener

For bread recipes, sugar is the most common sweetener. This includes granulated sugar and brown sugar. You can swap in raw sugar if you prefer it. Honey is also a common sweetener. Sugars (including honey) don't technically expire, but they can become contaminated. Keep them in well-sealed containers out of direct sunlight. As you experiment with different bread recipes, you might see calls for alternative sweeteners like coconut sugar, agave, date sugar, and so on.

Having the right ingredients on hand means you can bake bread whenever you feel like it. Essentials include flour, leavening, sweeteners, salt, and dairy. Extras like spices, nuts, and dried fruit make recipes more interesting.

Salt

You should already have salt in your pantry if you do any cooking or baking at all. Basic granulated table salt is really all you need, but if you want to elevate certain bread recipes (like pretzels), get coarse sea salt. This is a finishing salt, so it doesn't replace table salt. Sprinkle coarse salt on top of your breads. You can also mix seasoned salt (which includes paprika, onion powder, garlic powder, etc) with butter to spread on savory breads.

Eggs and dairy

Eggs are a binder, which is very important in bread-making. Choose large eggs when shopping. Most recipes are created with large eggs, and since baking is an exact science, you want to follow the recipes to the letter. When baking with eggs, always bring them to room temperature first. They mix into other ingredients more easily.

The other dairy ingredients you'll most likely need are butter and milk.

Unsalted butter is the way to go, unless the recipe asks for salted butter. Butter adds flavor and tenderness, which is why butter-heavy breads like brioche are so much softer than baguettes, which have no fat. You'll also want butter to spread on your fresh-baked creations. For quick breads made from batter, you'll need milk. Different variations of white bread - like milk bread - also use milk.

Olive oil

Every home cook or baker should have olive oil in their pantry. It's great for serving and dipping, but it's also used in certain recipes. It adds flavor and can replace butter in just about any bread recipe if you want.

Extracts and spices

You don't technically need extracts and spices, but they make homemade bread so much tastier. Use them to experiment with flavors, so you can make several variations of the same recipe. Vanilla, almond, and orange extract are delicious, while spices like cinnamon, ginger, nutmeg, and more are also great. These flavors are especially good for holidays like Christmas.

Add-ins

Think seeds, nuts, dried fruit, oats, chocolate, flaked coconut, and more. These can be easily added to recipes to make things more interesting. Nuts, seeds, and oats add nutrients as well as texture. Chocolate and dried fruit turn more basic bread recipes into something sweeter.

Must-have equipment

Once you have a good stock of ingredients, you'll need certain equipment to make the best bread possible. If you bake already, you most likely have some of the essentials. Some bread-specific tools can be very helpful.

Mixing bowl/plastic tub

Depending on the type of bread you're making, you'll want either a mixing bowl or a plastic tub. For batters, a regular mixing bowl is fine. For dough, a tub is a bit better. It's also easier to shape the dough into leaves since the bottom of the tub is flat. You can keep the dough in the tub to rise, too.

Dough scraper

Many bread recipes ask you to divide up dough. A dough scraper (also called a pastry scraper or bench knife) makes it easy to cut up dough, shape your loaves, and scrape dough that gets stuck.

Kitchen scale

A lot of bread recipes measure by grams. This is because measuring by cups can get you very different amounts, depending on how packed the ingredients are. Weighing your flour lets you be more precise and consistent. You'll end up with better results.

Loaf pan

If you want to make quick breads or breads that have a "weaker" dough (like rye), you'll need a loaf pan to hold it together. You can find loaf pans in just about every size. In the US, the standard loaf pan measures 8.5 x 4.5 x 2.5 inches.

> **Baking bread is much easier when you have the right tools and equipment. If you don't have things like a dough hook, loaf pan, or kitchen scale already, consider buying them before trying your first bread recipe.**

Dough hook

The regular attachment on your stand mixer might not work that well for sticky bread doughs. A dough hook is a better choice.

Dough whisk

You can usually use a mixer to get your doughs together, but sometimes it's better to do it by hand. A dough whisk is much better than a wooden spoon. It brings the dough together faster.

Quick-read thermometer

You might think a kitchen thermometer's only use is for meat or candy, but it can be useful for bread-making, as well. With yeasted breads, fermentation and temperature are linked. Knowing what temperature your dough is and seeing how it acts can help you make better bread.

Indoor thermometer

The temperature of your kitchen has a big effect on a dough's ability to rise well. Yeast likes warmth and humidity. Between 75-78 degrees is the ideal temperature with high humidity. An indoor thermometer lets you monitor the room.

Dough-rising bucket

Dough-rising buckets are a great way to trap humidity and watch your dough's rise. These use food-safe plastic and are very affordable.

Bread knife

When your bread is ready to eat, a good bread knife gets you nice slices. Look for a sharp one that's longer than 7 inches. Serrated knives were made specifically for bread, so those will work best. They let you saw through loaves without squishing them.

Chapter 4: Top Bread-Making Tips and Problem Solving

Bread-making has a bit of a learning curve depending on how experienced you are and the type of recipe you're trying out. Like all baking, bread-making is an exact science. Mistakes are just part of the process. That being said, there are things you can remember to stay on track. In this chapter, I'll go over a handful of tips and solutions to common problems.

Tips for bread-baking success

Before picking a bread recipe and jumping in, keep these five tips in mind. Since they are general tips, they can apply to just about every bread type and recipe you have your eye on.

Tip #1: Follow the instructions

Bread-making is not the time to do your own thing. If you've baked at all before, you most likely understand the importance of following a recipe. Slight deviations from a recipe can produce drastically different results. Baking is a science. Read the recipe carefully and follow it to the letter.

Tip #2: Start out with an easy bread

If you're baking bread for the first time, start out with something easy. There's less room for error and you're more likely to end up with something that looks and tastes good. This builds your confidence. There are countless recipes out there for simple no-knead breads. Focaccia and challah are also fairly easy. Sourdough is known to be a little harder, so if you really want to try it, work your way up from easier breads first.

Tip #3: Make sure you have all the right ingredients and set them out before starting

When you're considering a recipe, check to make sure you have all the right ingredients. If it uses yeast, make sure you have the right type of yeast. Before diving in, set out all your ingredients on your workstation. Bring refrigerated ingredients like butter and eggs to room temperature. Getting everything out makes the process smoother and faster. You won't need to disrupt your flow by hunting for an ingredient in the pantry.

Tip #4: Use a scale

In the must-have equipment section, I talked about getting a scale. If you were thinking maybe you would skip that tool, reconsider. Digital scales are not expensive and they can make a really big difference in how your bread turns out. You'll have way more control when you measure by weight and not volume.

Tip #5: Focus on kneading

Many bread recipes will require kneading. Beginners are often surprised by how hard kneading is and how long it takes. Under-kneading is way more common than over-kneading, especially for beginners. If you don't knead the dough enough, your bread can collapse in the oven. The texture ends up dense. Watch videos of the proper technique for kneading and set a timer for the recommended amount of time. Prepare for a workout.

> **New to bread baking? Try easy breads first, like focaccia or challah. Many white or wheat sandwich bread recipes are also pretty easy.**

Tips for problem solving

When you start baking bread, there are certain problems you'll likely face at one time or another. How do you deal with them? Here are five of the most common and what they mean:

Problem #1: Dough didn't rise

If your dough failed to rise - or rose very slowly - there are a few possible reasons why. The first is that the room temperature wasn't right. Yeast needs warmth and humidity. Another possibility is that the yeast expired or you didn't use enough. Before baking, always check the "best by" date on the yeast and measure carefully. Check the temperature of your liquids, too. If liquids were too hot or too cold, the dough won't rise properly. The use of too much salt and/or sugar can also mess up your dough's rise.

Problem #2: Your bread collapsed in the oven

The first thing to do if you notice your bread collapsing is to check the oven temperature. If it isn't hot enough, the bread will collapse. Always preheat the oven before putting bread in. Another explanation is that the flour you used was too weak. If you follow recipe recommendations for flours and the recipe is good, this most likely won't be the issue. Don't substitute other flours for bread flour. Bread flour has a higher amount of protein, which holds the bread together. If the recipe asked for all-purpose flour and the bread is collapsing, swap in a little bit of bread flour next time you make the bread.

Problem #3: The inside of your bread is gummy

If your bread has a gummy texture when you cut into it, there are two possible reasons why. The first is that the oven temperature was too hot. This caused the outside of the bread to cook too quickly, leaving the inside underdone. The other reason is that you simply didn't leave the bread in the oven long enough. If this is the case, you can probably save the bread by baking it a little longer. If the outside is already too brown, however, putting it back in the oven likely won't work.

Problem #4: The bread is really dry

You took your bread out of the oven and let it cool, but it's already really dry. What happened? If you substituted in whole-grain flour to make the recipe healthier, this is why it's dry. Whole-grain flour is more absorbent, which is why recipes that use it call for more liquid. If you're swapping out another type of flour, you need to add more liquid. The other reason for dryness is that the flour you used didn't have enough protein. Avoid swapping out bread flour, which has a higher protein count. Bread flour keeps the bread moist.

Problem #5: The bread is crumbly

Crumbly, coarse bread is not an unusual problem. There are a handful of explanations. The first is that the dough wasn't kneaded enough. You want a beautifully-smooth dough with a slightly "tacky" feel. It should spring back when you poke it and stretch without tearing. Another reason for crumbly bread is that the oven isn't hot enough or you let the dough rise too much. If you put in too much flour, the bread will end up crumbly, too. Use a kitchen scale to avoid this issue.

Baking really good bread requires patience and practice. There will be mistakes made along the way, but these are important learning experiences. Avoid future errors by following tips and understanding what happened when things go wrong.

LOAVES

French Bread

Serves: 12 / Preparation time: 10 minutes / Cooking time: 1 hour 30 minutes

1 egg, lightly beaten

2 ½ cups all-purpose flour

1 tbsp olive oil

1 tbsp granulated sugar

2 tsp active dry yeast

1 cup warm water

1 tsp salt

- Add yeast, warm water, and sugar in a bowl of the stand mixer and let sit for 5 minutes or until foamy.
- Mix in flour, oil, and salt on low speed until well combined and sticky dough is forms.
- Place dough in a greased bowl and let rise for 50 minutes.
- Roll dough into a 9*13-inch rectangle and then roll up into a long roll.
- Preheat the oven to 375 F/ 190 C. Line baking sheet with parchment paper.
- Place rolled dough onto the prepared baking sheet. Make 4-5 slits on top of dough roll 2-3-inch apart. Let rise 1 hour.
- Bake in preheated oven for 20-25 minutes. Brush egg onto the top of loaf and bake for 2-3 minutes more.
- Slice and serve.

Per Serving: Calories: 116; Total Fat: 1.8g; Saturated Fat: 0.3g; Protein: 3.4g; Carbs: 21.2g; Fiber: 0.8g; Sugar: 1.1g

Flavorful Cheddar Cheese Loaf

Serves: 8 / Preparation time: 10 minutes / Cooking time: 45 minutes

1 egg, lightly beaten

1 tbsp butter, melted

1 cup milk

1 ½ cups cheddar cheese, shredded

¼ tsp dry mustard

½ tsp oregano, crushed

1 tbsp sugar

4 tsp baking powder

2 cups all-purpose flour

½ tsp garlic salt

- Preheat the oven to 350 F/ 180 C. Grease 8*4-inch loaf pan and set aside.
- In a large bowl, mix together flour, mustard, oregano, sugar, baking powder, and salt. Add cheddar cheese and mix well.
- In a small bowl, whisk eggs with butter, and milk.
- Pour egg mixture into the flour mixture and mix until just combined.
- Pour mixture into the prepared loaf pan and bake for 45 minutes.
- Slice and serve.

Per Serving: Calories: 244; Total Fat: 10g; Saturated Fat: 6g; Protein: 10.3g; Carbs: 28.6g; Fiber: 1g; Sugar: 3.2g

Zucchini Bread

Serves: 16 / Preparation time: 10 minutes / Cooking time: 60 minutes

3 eggs

1 tsp vanilla

2 cups grated zucchini

2 tsp lemon zest

¼ tsp baking powder

3 cups all-purpose flour

2 cups sugar

1 tbsp fresh lemon juice

6 oz yogurt

1 cup canola oil

1 tsp salt

- Preheat the oven to 350 F/ 180 C. Grease two 8.5*4.5-inch bread pan and set aside.
- In a mixing bowl, whisk together oil, sugar, lemon juice, and yogurt until just combined. Add egg one by one and beat well.
- In a separate bowl, mix together flour, baking soda, baking powder, and salt. Add lemon zest and stir well.
- Add flour mixture into the oil mixture and mix until just combined.
- Add vanilla and zucchini and stir well.
- Divide batter evenly between prepared bread pans and bake for 55-60 minutes.
- Slice and serve.

Per Serving: Calories: 322; Total Fat: 14.9 g; Saturated Fat: 1.4g; Protein: 4.3g; Carbs: 44.3g; Fiber: 0.8g; Sugar: 26.2g

Simple Lemon Bread

Serves: 12 / Preparation time: 10 minutes / Cooking time: 1 hour 15 minutes

3 eggs

¾ cup milk

¾ cup butter, softened

1 ¼ cups granulated sugar

1 ½ tsp baking powder

2 ¼ cups flour

1 tbsp lemon zest, grated

¾ tsp salt

- Preheat the oven to 350 F/ 180 C. Grease 9*5-inch loaf pan and set aside.
- In a mixing bowl, mix together flour, sugar, baking powder, salt, and butter until mixture resembles coarse crumbs. Add lemon zest and stir well.
- In a small bowl, whisk eggs with milk until combined.
- Pour egg mixture into the flour mixture and mix until just combined.
- Pour mixture into the prepared loaf pan and bake for 1 hour 15 minutes.
- Slice and serve.

Per Serving: Calories: 289; Total Fat: 13.1g; Saturated Fat: 7.9g; Protein: 4.4g; Carbs: 40g; Fiber: 0.7g; Sugar: 21.7g

Soft & Moist Banana Bread

Serves: 12 / Preparation time: 10 minutes / Cooking time: 55 minutes

2 eggs

½ tsp cinnamon

1 tsp baking soda

1 cup granulated sugar

2 cups all-purpose flour

1 tsp vanilla

3 ripe bananas

1 stick butter

½ tsp salt

- Preheat the oven to 350 F/ 180 C. Grease 9*5-inch loaf pan and set aside.
- Add butter to a large bowl and microwave until melted. Add bananas to the melted butter and mash with a fork.
- Add eggs and vanilla and stir until well combined.
- In a separate bowl, mix together flour, cinnamon, baking soda, sugar, and salt.
- Add flour mixture to the egg mixture and mix until just combined.
- Pour batter into the prepared loaf pan and bake in preheated oven for 45-55 minutes.
- Slice and serve.

Per Serving: Calories: 244; Total Fat: 8.7g; Saturated Fat: 5.1g; Protein: 3.5g; Carbs: 39.5g; Fiber: 1.4g; Sugar: 20.5g

Jalapeno Cheddar Bread

Serves: 10 / Preparation time: 10 minutes / Cooking time: 50 minutes

3 cups all-purpose flour

¼ cup butter, melted

1 ½ cups buttermilk

3 jalapeno peppers, chopped

8 oz cheddar cheese, shredded

½ tsp ground white pepper

1 ½ tbsp baking powder

2 tbsp sugar

1 ¼ tsp salt

- Preheat the oven to 375 F/ 190 C. Grease 9*5-inch loaf pan and set aside.
- In a large mixing bowl, mix together flour, baking powder, sugar, white pepper, and salt. Add jalapenos and cheese and stir to combine.
- Whisk butter and buttermilk together and add to the flour mixture. Stir until just combined.
- Pour batter into the prepared loaf pan and bake for 45-50 minutes.
- Slice and serve.

Per Serving: Calories: 297; Total Fat: 12.9g; Saturated Fat: 8g; Protein: 10.9g; Carbs: 34.5g; Fiber: 1.3g; Sugar: 4.5g

Lemon Poppy Seed Bread loaf

Serves: 12 / Preparation time: 10 minutes / Cooking time: 50 minutes

6 eggs

3 tbsp butter, melted

2 tbsp fresh lemon juice

2 lemon zest

2 tbsp poppy seeds

½ cup sukrin

½ tsp baking powder

9.5 oz almond flour

- Preheat the oven to 350 F/ 180 C. Grease 9*5-inch loaf pan and set aside.
- In a large mixing bowl, mix together almond flour, poppy seeds, sweetener, and baking powder.
- Add butter, lemon juice, and lemon zest and mix well.
- Add eggs and mix until just combined.
- Pour batter into the prepared loaf pan and bake in preheated oven for 45-50 minutes.
- Slice and serve.

Per Serving: Calories: 201; Total Fat: 17g; Saturated Fat: 4g; Protein: 9g; Carbs: 6g; Fiber: 3g; Sugar: 1g

Banana Strawberry Bread

Serves: 12 / Preparation time: 10 minutes / Cooking time: 60 minutes

2 eggs

½ cup walnuts, choppefd

¾ cup strawberries, diced

1 cup mashed banana

¼ cup yogurt

½ cup granulated sugar

½ tsp baking powder

½ tsp baking soda

1 tsp cinnamon

1 ½ cups all-purpose flour

¼ tsp salt

- Preheat the oven to 350 F/ 180 C. Line loaf pan with parchment paper and set aside.
- In a large mixing bowl, mix together flour, baking powder, baking soda, cinnamon, and salt and set aside.
- In a separate bowl, whisk together eggs, mashed banana, yogurt, and sugar until well combined. Add walnuts and strawberries and fold well.
- Add flour mixture into the egg mixture and mix until just combined.
- Pour batter into the prepared loaf pan and bake for 50-60 minutes.
- Slice and serve.

Per Serving: Calories: 149; Total Fat: 4.1g; Saturated Fat: 0.5g; Protein: 4.3g; Carbs: 25g; Fiber: 1.4g; Sugar: 10.8g

Orange Bread Loaf

Serves: 10 / Preparation time: 10 minutes / Cooking time: 50 minutes

4 eggs

2 tsp baking powder

2 cups all-purpose flour

1 tsp vanilla

4 oz butter, softened

1 cup fresh orange juice

1 orange zest

1 cup sugar

- Preheat the oven to 350 F/ 180 C. Grease 9*5-inch loaf pan and set aside.
- In a large bowl, whisk eggs and sugar until creamy. Whisk in vanilla, butter, orange juice, and orange zest.
- Add flour and baking powder and fold until incorporated.
- Pour batter into the loaf pan and bake for 50 minutes.
- Slice and serve.

Per Serving: Calories: 286; Total Fat: 11.3g; Saturated Fat: 6.4g; Protein: 5.1g; Carbs: 42.3g; Fiber: 0.8g; Sugar: 22.4g

Fluffy Pumpkin Bread

Serves: 12 / Preparation time: 10 minutes / Cooking time: 1 hour 5 minutes

2 eggs

½ cup walnuts, chopped

½ cup applesauce

15 oz can pumpkin

½ tsp baking powder

2 tsp cinnamon

1 tsp baking soda

½ cup brown sugar

1 cup sugar

1 2/3 cup all-purpose flour

¾ tsp salt

- Preheat the oven to 350 F/ 180 C. Grease 9*5-inch loaf pan and set aside.
- In a large mixing bowl, mix together all dry ingredients.
- In a separate bowl, whisk eggs with applesauce and pumpkin.
- Add dry ingredients mixture into the egg mixture and mix until just combined. Add walnuts and fold well.
- Pour batter into the prepared loaf pan and bake for 65-70 minutes.
- Once done, then allow to cool for 10 minutes.
- Slice and serve.

Per Serving: Calories: 209; Total Fat: 4.1g; Saturated Fat: 0.5g; Protein: 4.4g; Carbs: 40.9g; Fiber: 2.2g; Sugar: 24.9g

Barley Bread

Serves: 16 / Preparation time: 10 minutes / Cooking time: 40 minutes

2 eggs

3 tbsp honey

1/3 cup olive oil

1 ½ cups buttermilk

½ tsp baking soda

2 tbsp baking powder

3 cups barley flour

1 ¼ tsp salt

- Preheat the oven to 350 F/ 180 C. Grease 8.5*4.5-inch loaf pan and set aside.
- In a large bowl, mix together flour, baking powder, baking soda, and salt.
- In a separate bowl, whisk eggs with honey, oil, and buttermilk.
- Add egg mixture into the flour mixture and stir until just combined.
- Pour batter into the prepared loaf pan and bake for 35-40 minutes.
- Slice and serve.

Per Serving: Calories: 163; Total Fat: 5.4g; Saturated Fat: 1g; Protein: 4.4g; Carbs: 26g; Fiber: 2.9g; Sugar: 4.6g

Cranberry Cream Cheese Bread

Serves: 16 / Preparation time: 10 minutes / Cooking time: 60 minutes

4 eggs

2 cups cranberries

1 ½ tsp baking powder

2 cups all-purpose flour

1 ½ tsp vanilla

1 ½ cups sugar

8 oz cream cheese, softened

1 cup butter, softened

½ tsp salt

- Preheat the oven to 350 F/ 180 C. Grease two 9*5-inch loaf pan and set aside.
- In a large bowl, cream together cream cheese, butter, vanilla, and sugar. Add eggs one at a time and beat until combined.
- In a separate bowl, mix together flour, baking powder, and salt.
- Add flour mixture into the cream cheese mixture and mix until just combined. Add cranberries and fold well.
- Pour batter into the prepared loaf pans and bake for 60 minutes.
- Slice and serve.

Per Serving: Calories: 303; Total Fat: 17.7g; Saturated Fat: 10.8g; Protein: 4.2g; Carbs: 32.7g; Fiber: 0.9g; Sugar: 19.5g

Blueberry Bread

Serves: 12 / Preparation time: 10 minutes / Cooking time: 55 minutes

2 eggs

3 tbsp lemon zest, grated

¾ cup blueberries

¼ cup fresh lemon juice

¼ cup coconut oil, melted

¼ cup yogurt

½ cup maple syrup

1 tsp baking powder

1 ¾ cups all-purpose flour

½ tsp salt

- Preheat the oven to 350 F/ 180 C. Grease 8*4-inch loaf pan and set aside.
- In a small bowl, mix together flour, baking powder, and salt.
- In a large mixing bowl, beat eggs with lemon juice, coconut oil, maple syrup, and yogurt. Add flour mixture into the egg mixture and mix until just combined.
- Add blueberries and lemon zest and fold well.
- Pour batter into the prepared loaf pan and bake for 45-55 minutes.
- Slice and serve.

Per Serving: Calories: 162; Total Fat: 5.6g; Saturated Fat: 4.3g; Protein: 3.2g; Carbs: 25.1g; Fiber: 0.8g; Sugar: 9.4g

Moist Apple Cinnamon Bread

Serves: 10 / Preparation time: 10 minutes / Cooking time: 60 minutes

3 apples, peeled and chopped

1 ½ cups yogurt

¾ cup vegetable oil

1 tsp vanilla

2 eggs

¼ tsp ground nutmeg

½ tsp ground ginger

2 tsp ground cinnamon

½ tsp baking soda

2 tsp baking powder

1 ¼ cups brown sugar

3 cups all-purpose flour

½ tsp salt

- Preheat the oven to 350 F/ 180 C. Grease 9*5-inch loaf pan and set aside.
- In a mixing bowl, mix together flour, baking soda, baking powder, sugar, spices, and salt.
- In a separate bowl, whisk eggs with yogurt, oil, and vanilla until smooth.
- Add flour mixture into the egg mixture and mix until just combined.
- Add apple and fold well. Pour batter into the prepared loaf pan and bake for 60 minutes.
- Slice and serve.

Per Serving: Calories: 427; Total Fat: 18.2g; Saturated Fat: 3.9g; Protein: 7.3g; Carbs: 59.3g; Fiber: 2.9g; Sugar: 27.4g

Zucchini Chocolate Bread

Serves: 10 / Preparation time: 10 minutes / Cooking time: 60 minutes

2 eggs

¾ cup chocolate chips

1/3 cup cocoa powder

1 tsp baking soda

1 ½ cup all-purpose flour

1 ½ tsp vanilla

½ cup butter, melted

¼ cup coconut sugar

¼ cup maple syrup

1 ¾ cup zucchini, grated & squeeze out excess liquid

½ tsp salt

- Preheat the oven to 350 F/ 180 C. Grease 9*5-inch loaf pan and set aside.
- In a large bowl, whisk eggs with vanilla, butter, maple syrup, and coconut sugar.
- In a separate bowl, mix together flour, cocoa powder, baking soda, and salt.
- Add flour mixture to the egg mixture and mix until well combined.
- Add chocolate chips and grated zucchini and stir until just combined.
- Pour batter into the prepared loaf pan and bake for 50-60 minutes.
- Slice and serve.

Per Serving: Calories: 280; Total Fat: 14.4g; Saturated Fat: 9g; Protein: 4.9g; Carbs: 34.4g; Fiber: 2g; Sugar: 16.6g

Healthy Zucchini Bread

Serves: 8 / Preparation time: 10 minutes / Cooking time: 45 minutes

1 egg

¼ cup chocolate chips

1 tsp baking soda

1 ½ tsp baking powder

¼ tsp ginger

¼ tsp nutmeg

1 tsp cinnamon

2 cups oat flour

1 cup grated zucchini, squeezed out excess liquid

½ cup almond milk

½ cup honey

2 tsp vanilla

1 tbsp olive oil

¼ tsp salt

- Preheat the oven to 350 F/ 180 C. Grease 8*4-inch loaf pan and set aside.
- In a large bowl, whisk egg, almond milk, honey, vanilla, olive oil, and zucchini.
- Add oat flour, baking soda, baking powder, spices, and salt and stir until well combined.
- Add chocolate chip and fold well.
- Pour batter into the prepared loaf pan and bake for 40-45 minutes.
- Slice and serve.

Per Serving: Calories: 247; Total Fat: 9g; Saturated Fat: 5.1g; Protein: 4.7g;

Carbs: 38.5g; Fiber: 3.1g; Sugar: 21g

Perfect Pumpkin Bread

Serves: 12 / Preparation time: 10 minutes / Cooking time: 55 minutes

2 eggs

1/8 tsp ground ginger

¼ tsp ground cloves

½ tsp ground nutmeg

½ tsp ground cinnamon

1 tsp baking soda

1 ¾ cups flour

1 ½ cups sugar

1/3 cup water

½ cup vegetable oil

8 oz pumpkin puree

¾ tsp salt

- Preheat the oven to 350 F/ 180 C. Grease loaf pan and set aside.
- In a bowl, whisk eggs, sugar, water, oil, and pumpkin puree until combined.
- In a separate bowl, mix dry ingredients.
- Add dry ingredient mixture into the egg mixture and mix until just combined.
- Pour batter into the prepared loaf pan and bake for 50-55 minutes.
- Slice and serve.

Per Serving: Calories: 258; Total Fat: 10.1g; Saturated Fat: 2.1g; Protein: 3g; Carbs: 40.7g; Fiber: 1.1g; Sugar: 25.8g

Vegan Pumpkin Bread

Serves: 12 / Preparation time: 10 minutes / Cooking time: 50 minutes

1 ¼ cup pumpkin puree

1 cup pecans, chopped

1/8 tsp cloves

¼ tsp ginger

¼ tsp nutmeg

1 tsp cinnamon

1 tsp baking soda

1 cup all-purpose flour

¾ cup whole wheat flour

1 tsp vanilla

1 tsp apple cider vinegar

¼ cup almond milk

1/3 cup coconut oil, melted

¾ cup sugar

½ tsp salt

- Preheat the oven to 350 F/ 180 C. Grease 9*5-inch loaf pan and set aside.
- In a mixing bowl, whisk together pumpkin, vanilla, vinegar, milk, oil, and sugar and set aside.
- In a separate bowl, mix together flours, spices, baking soda, and salt.
- Add flour mixture into the pumpkin mixture and mix until just combined.
- Pour batter into the prepared loaf pan and top with chopped pecans.
- Bake for 50 minutes.
- Slice and serve.

Per Serving: Calories: 263; Total Fat: 15g; Saturated Fat: 7.1g; Protein: 3.9g; Carbs: 31.6g; Fiber: 3.5g; Sugar: 14g

Banana Oatmeal Bread

Serves: 16 / Preparation time: 10 minutes / Cooking time: 55 minutes

1 egg

1 2/3 cup rolled oats

½ tsp ground nutmeg

2/3 tsp ground cinnamon

4 ripe bananas

2 egg whites

1 tbsp canola oil

¼ tsp baking powder

½ tsp baking soda

½ cup brown sugar

1 ¼ cup all-purpose flour

½ tsp salt

- Preheat the oven to 350 F/ 180 C. Line loaf pan with parchment paper and set aside.
- In a large bowl, mix together flour, baking powder, baking soda, and salt.
- In a separate bowl, mash bananas with a fork.
- Add eggs and oil into the flour mixture and mix well.
- Add bananas, nutmeg, and cinnamon in flour mixture and beat using a hand mixer for 1-2 minutes.
- Add rolled oats and fold well.
- Pour batter into the prepared loaf pan and bake for 45-55 minutes.
- Slice and serve.

Per Serving: Calories: 126; Total Fat: 2g; Saturated Fat: 0.3g; Protein: 3.3g; Carbs: 24.6g; Fiber: 2g; Sugar: 8.2g

Banana Chocolate Chip Bread

Serves: 10 / Preparation time: 10 minutes / Cooking time: 50 minutes

2 eggs

½ cup chocolate chips

1 ½ cups all-purpose flour

1 tsp baking soda

1 tsp vanilla

1 cup granulated sugar

½ cup sour cream

½ cup butter, melted

3 ripe bananas

1 tsp salt

- Preheat the oven to 350 F/ 180 C. Grease 9*8-inch loaf pan and set aside.
- In a large mixing bowl, add bananas and mash using a fork until smooth. Stir in sour cream and melted butter.
- Add eggs, vanilla, sugar, and salt and stir well.
- Add flour, baking soda, and salt and stir until just combined. Add chocolate chips and fold well.
- Pour batter into the prepared loaf pan and bake for 50-60 minutes.
- Slice and serve.

Per Serving: Calories: 339; Total Fat: 15.3g; Saturated Fat: 9.4g; Protein: 4.5g; Carbs: 48g; Fiber: 1.7g; Sugar: 28.9g

Delicious Mango Bread

Serves: 12 / Preparation time: 10 minutes / Cooking time: 60 minutes

1 egg

¼ cup walnuts, chopped

¼ cup coconut

1 ½ cups mango, diced

½ tsp vanilla

½ cup white sugar

¼ cup vegetable oil

¼ cup butter, softened

1 tsp cinnamon

1 tsp baking soda

1 cup all-purpose flour

¼ tsp salt

- Preheat the oven to 350 F/ 180 C. Grease loaf pan and set aside.
- In a large bowl, mix together flour, cinnamon, baking soda, and salt.
- In a separate bowl, cream together sugar, oil, and butter. Add egg and vanilla and beat until well combined.
- Add flour mixture into the wet mixture and stir until just combined.
- Add walnuts, coconut, and mango to the batter and fold well.
- Pour batter into the prepared loaf pan and bake for 50-60 minutes.
- Slice and serve.

Per Serving: Calories: 184; Total Fat: 11g; Saturated Fat: 4.1g; Protein: 2.5g; Carbs: 20.1g; Fiber: 1g; Sugar: 11.4g

Olive Feta Bread

Serves: 10 / Preparation time: 10 minutes / Cooking time: 50 minutes

5 Egg whites

2 Egg yolks

2 tbsp Psyllium husk powder

5 sun-dried tomatoes

1/2 cup olives

2.5 oz feta cheese

1 tbsp dried oregano

2 cups flaxseed flour

4 tbsp coconut oil

1 tbsp baking powder

2 tbsp apple cider vinegar

1 tbsp dried thyme

1/2 cup boiling water

1/2 tsp Salt

- Preheat the oven to 350 F/ 180 C. Grease loaf pan and set aside.
- In a large bowl, mix together Psyllium husk powder, baking powder, and flaxseed.
- Add oil and eggs and mix until well combined. Add vinegar and stir well.
- Add boiling water and stir to combine.
- Add tomatoes, olives, and feta cheese and mix well.
- Pour batter into the prepared loaf pan and bake for 50 minutes.
- Slice and serve.

Per Serving: Calories: 226; Total Fat: 16.8g; Saturated Fat: 6.2g; Protein:

8.8g; Carbs: 14.1g; Fiber: 9.1g; Sugar: 2.1g

Apple Zucchini Bread

Serves: 10 / Preparation time: 10 minutes / Cooking time: 50 minutes

2 eggs

1/2 cup applesauce

1/4 cup coconut sugar

1 tsp ground cinnamon

1/2 cup apple, grated

1 1/2 cups zucchini, grated

1 tsp vanilla extract

1/4 cup yogurt

1/2 tsp baking soda

1/2 tsp baking powder

1 1/2 cups whole wheat flour

1/4 tsp sea salt

- Preheat the oven to 350 F/ 180 C. Grease 9*5-inch loaf pan and set aside.
- In a large bowl, mix together flour, cinnamon, salt, baking soda, and baking powder.
- In a separate bowl, whisk eggs, coconut sugar, vanilla, yogurt, and applesauce.
- Add flour mixture into the wet mixture and stir until just combined.
- Add apples and zucchini and fold well.
- Pour batter into the prepared loaf pan and bake for 40-50 minutes.
- Slice and serve.

Per Serving: Calories: 119; Total Fat: 1.2g; Saturated Fat: 0.4g; Protein: 3.7g; Carbs: 23.5g; Fiber: 1.3g; Sugar: 8.1g

Herb Cheddar Cheese Bread

Serves: 10 / Preparation time: 10 minutes / Cooking time: 40 minutes

1 egg

1 3/4 cups flour

1 1/2 cups cheddar cheese, shredded

1 tbsp fresh basil, chopped

4 tbsp butter

1/2 tsp garlic powder

1 cup milk

1 tbsp fresh thyme, chopped

1 tbsp fresh parsley, chopped

1/4 tsp ground pepper

2 tsp baking powder

1/2 tsp salt

- Preheat the oven to 400 F/ 200 C. Grease 9*5-inch loaf pan and set aside.
- In a mixing bowl, mix together flour, garlic powder, baking powder, pepper, and salt.
- Add butter and using fork mix until mixture is crumbly.
- Add milk, egg, and fresh herbs and mix well. Stir in cheese.
- Transfer mixture into the greased loaf pan and bake for 35-40 minutes.
- Slice and serve.

Per Serving: Calories: 210; Total Fat: 11.4g; Saturated Fat: 7g; Protein: 8g; Carbs: 19g; Fiber: 0.7g; Sugar: 1.3g

Bacon Jalapeno Pepper Bread

Serves: 6 / Preparation time: 10 minutes / Cooking time: 50 minutes

6 eggs

1/2 cup olive oil

1/2 cup coconut flour

4 oz bacon, sliced

1/4 tsp baking soda

1/4 cup water

3 jalapeno pepper, chopped

1/2 tsp sea salt

- Preheat the oven to 400 F/ 200 C. Greased loaf pan and set aside.
- Roast bacon & jalapeno in preheated oven for 10 minutes.
- Add bacon and jalapeno in food processor and process until just-chopped.
- In a large bowl, whisk eggs, baking soda, sea salt, coconut flour, oil, and water.
- Add jalapeno and bacon and fold well.
- Pour batter into the greased loaf pan and bake at 375 F for 40 minutes.
- Slice and serve.

Per Serving: Calories: 316; Total Fat: 29.3g; Saturated Fat: 6.5g; Protein: 12.8g; Carbs: 1.7g; Fiber: 0.6g; Sugar: 0.7g

Easy No Yeast Bread

Serves: 8 / Preparation time: 10 minutes / Cooking time: 35 minutes

½ cup yogurt

¼ cup olive oil

1 ½ cups all-purpose flour

1 tsp baking powder

½ tsp salt

- Line baking sheet with parchment paper and set aside.
- In a mixing bowl, whisk together yogurt, olive oil, baking powder, and salt.
- Slowly add flour in yogurt mixture and mix until sticky dough forms.
- Roll dough into a log and place onto a prepared baking sheet. Lightly brush with oil.
- Bake at 350 F/ 180 C for 25-35 minutes.
- Slice and serve.

Per Serving: Calories: 151; Total Fat: 6.7g; Saturated Fat: 1.1g; Protein: 3.3g; Carbs: 19.3g; Fiber: 0.6g; Sugar: 1.1g

Herb Bread

Serves: 12 / Preparation time: 10 minutes / Cooking time: 1 hour 20 minutes

12 eggs

1 1/2 tbsp olive oil

1/2 cup almond milk

2 1/2 tbsp apple cider vinegar

1 tbsp dried sage

1 1/2 tsp dried thyme

2 tsp garlic powder

1 cup coconut flour

1 cup flaxseed meal

1/4 cup whole psyllium husk flakes

4 tsp baking powder

2 tbsp dried rosemary, crumbled

1 1/2 tsp kosher salt

- Preheat the oven to 325 F/ 162 C. Greased loaf pan and set aside.
- In a large bowl, mix together garlic powder, herbs, salt, baking powder, psyllium husk flakes, flaxseed meal, and coconut flour. Set aside.
- In a separate bowl, beat eggs until frothy.
- Add apple cider vinegar, almond milk, and oil into the egg and beat until well combined.
- Slowly add dry ingredients and beat until just combined.
- Pour batter into the prepared loaf pan and bake for 80 minutes.
- Slice and serve.

Per Serving: Calories: 170; Total Fat: 11.7g; Saturated Fat: 4.3g; Protein: 7.8g; Carbs: 7.6g; Fiber: 5.3g; Sugar: 1g

Whole Wheat Bread

Serves: 12 / Preparation time: 10 minutes / Cooking time: 40 minutes

3 3/4 cups whole wheat flour

3 tbsp butter

1 1/2 cups warm water

1/2 tsp kosher salt

1/4 oz active dry yeast

1/4 cup honey

- Grease 9*5-inch loaf pan and set aside.
- In a large bowl, mix warm water and yeast and set aside for 5 minutes
- Add butter and honey and stir well.
- Add flour and salt and mix until dough forms.
- Transfer dough onto a lightly floured surface and knead the dough for 10 minutes or until smooth.
- Shape dough into a ball and place into the greased bowl.
- Cover the bowl and let the dough rise about 45 minutes.
- Punch down the dough and transfer into the greased loaf pan.
- Cover loaf pan and let the dough rise for 30 minutes more.
- Preheat the oven to 350 F/ 180 C.
- Remove cover from the dough and bake a loaf for 40-45 minutes.
- Slice and serve.

Per Serving: Calories: 191; Total Fat: 3.3g; Saturated Fat: 1.9g; Protein: 4.3g; Carbs: 35.9g; Fiber: 1.2g; Sugar: 5.9g

Easy Sandwich Bread

Serves: 6 / Preparation time: 10 minutes / Cooking time: 35 minutes

2 cups all-purpose flour

3/4 cup warm water

2 tbsp butter

1 tbsp honey

1/4 cup milk powder

1 tsp instant yeast

1/2 tsp salt

- In a large bowl, mix together flour, milk powder, yeast, butter, sugar, and salt.
- Add warm water and mix until dough forms.
- Transfer dough onto the lightly floured surface and knead the dough for 5 minutes.
- Transfer dough into the greased bowl.
- Cover bowl and let the dough rise about 2 hours.
- Once the dough is doubled in size then knead the dough for 5 minutes.
- Roll dough into a 9-inch log.
- Grease 9*4-inch loaf pan.
- Transfer dough into the greased loaf pan. Cover the loaf pan and let the dough rise for 1 hour.
- Preheat the oven to 350 F/ 180 C.
- Bake a loaf for 30-35 minutes.
- Slice and serve.

Per Serving: Calories: 218; Total Fat: 4.3g; Saturated Fat: 2.5g; Protein: 6.6g; Carbs: 37.8g; Fiber: 1.3g; Sugar: 5.7g

Cinnamon Carrot Bread

Serves: 10 / Preparation time: 10 minutes / Cooking time: 50 minutes

1 egg

3/4 cup all-purpose flour

3/4 cup whole wheat flour

1 cup carrots, shredded

3/4 tsp vanilla

1/2 cup brown sugar

3/4 cup yogurt

3 tbsp vegetable oil

1 tsp baking soda

1 tsp baking powder

1/2 tsp nutmeg

1 1/2 tsp cinnamon

- Preheat the oven to 350 F/ 180 C. Grease 9*5-inch loaf pan and set aside.
- In a mixing bowl, mix together flours, baking powder, baking soda, and spices and set aside.
- In a separate bowl, whisk egg with vanilla, sugar, yogurt, and oil.
- Add carrots and stir well.
- Add flour mixture and stir until well combined.
- Pour mixture into the prepared loaf pan and bake for 50 minutes.
- Slice and serve.

Per Serving: Calories: 165; Total Fat: 5.1g; Saturated Fat: 1.2g; Protein: 4.3g; Carbs: 26g; Fiber: 2.2g; Sugar: 9.1g

Nut Orange Bread

Serves: 10 / Preparation time: 10 minutes / Cooking time: 60 minutes

1 egg, lightly beaten

3/4 cup sugar

4 tsp baking powder

3 cups flour

1/2 cup mixed nuts, chopped

3 tbsp shortening, melted

1 tbsp orange zest, grated

1 1/2 cups milk

1 tsp salt

- Preheat the oven to 375 F/ 190 C.
- In a large bowl, mix together flour, sugar, baking powder, and salt.
- In a separate bowl, whisk together egg, milk, and shortening.
- Add egg mixture into the flour mixture and stir until just combined.
- Add nuts and orange zest and fold well.
- Pour batter into the greased 4*8-inch loaf pan and bake for 1 hour.
- Slice and serve.

Per Serving: Calories: 298; Total Fat: 9.5g; Saturated Fat: 2.5g; Protein: 6.8g; Carbs: 48.1g; Fiber: 1.5g; Sugar: 17.1g

Mixed Nut Strawberry Bread

Serves: 24 / Preparation time: 10 minutes / Cooking time: 60 minutes

4 egg

16 oz frozen strawberries, thawed, drained, & lightly mashed

1 1/4 cups vegetable oil

2 cups sugar

1 cup mixed nuts, chopped

1 tsp baking soda

3 tsp cinnamon

3 cups all-purpose flour

1 tsp salt

- Preheat the oven to 350 F/ 190 C. Grease two 9*5-inch loaf pan and set aside.
- In a mixing bowl, whisk together oil and sugar. Add eggs and stir until well blended.
- Add remaining ingredients and stir until just combined.
- Pour batter into the prepared loaf pan and bake for 1 hour.
- Slice and serve.

Per Serving: Calories: 274; Total Fat: 15.6g; Saturated Fat: 3g; Protein: 3.5g; Carbs: 31.9g; Fiber: 1.3g; Sugar: 18.2g

Spelt Bread

Serves: 12 / Preparation time: 10 minutes / Cooking time: 60 minutes

4 cups spelt flour

1 1/4 cups mixed seeds

2 cups water

1/4 cup vinegar

1 tbsp honey

1.5 oz yeast

2 tsp salt

- Preheat the oven to 390 F/ 198 C.
- Add flour, salt, mixed seeds, and yeast into the large bowl and mix well.
- Add water, honey, and vinegar and mix until dough is formed.
- Transfer dough into the greased loaf pan and bake for 60 minutes.
- Slice and serve.

Per Serving: Calories: 152; Total Fat: 0.9g; Saturated Fat: 0.2g; Protein: 6.9g; Carbs: 31.9g; Fiber: 5.6g; Sugar: 1.6g

Nut & Seed Bread

Serves: 25 / Preparation time: 10 minutes / Cooking time: 25 minutes

5 eggs

1 cup flax seeds

1 cup chia seeds

1 cup pecans

1 cup walnuts

1 cup almonds

1 cup pumpkin seeds

1 cup sunflower seeds

1 tsp salt

- Line two small loaf pans with parchment paper and set aside.
- Preheat the oven to 425 F/ 218 C.
- In a large bowl, mix together all nuts and seeds.
- Add eggs and salt and stir until well combined.
- Pour mixture into the prepared loaf pans and bake for 25 minutes.
- Slice and serve.

Per Serving: Calories: 185; Total Fat: 15.6g; Saturated Fat: 1.8g; Protein: 7.1g; Carbs: 5.6g; Fiber: 2.9g; Sugar: 0.6g

BREADSTICKS

Delicious Breadsticks

Serves: 16 / Preparation time: 10 minutes / Cooking time: 18 minutes

1 egg

¼ cup sugar

3 ¼ cup flour

2 tbsp butter, softened

1 tbsp active dry yeast

1 cup warm water

1 tsp salt

For topping:

1 tsp Italian seasoning

3 tbsp butter, melted

- Add all ingredients except topping ingredients into the stand mixer bowl and mix using the dough hook until combined. Make sure the dough is soft and slightly sticky.
- Transfer dough onto the floured surface and knead 2-3 times and make ball.
- Cover dough and let rise 1 ½ hours.
- Roll dough onto the floured surface into a 12*15-inch rectangle. Using a pizza cutter slice into 16 pieces.
- Pinched the long side of each piece together to make a breadstick shape.
- Place prepared breadsticks pinched side down on a parchment-lined baking sheet. Cover and let rise for 30 minutes.
- Bake for 15-18 minutes at 350 F / 180 C.
- Brush breadstick with melted butter and sprinkle with Italian seasoning.
- Serve and enjoy.

Per Serving: Calories: 143; Total Fat: 4.2g; Saturated Fat: 2.4g; Protein: 3.3g;

Carbs: 22.9g; Fiber: 0.9g; Sugar: 3.3g

Italian Breadsticks

Serves: 16 / Preparation time: 10 minutes / Cooking time: 10 minutes

1 puff pastry sheet, thawed

2 tsp Italian seasoning

¼ cup parmesan cheese, grated

1 tbsp butter, melted

1 tsp garlic salt

- Unfold puff pastry sheet onto the lightly floured surface. Using a pizza cutter cut into thin strips.
- Brush puff pastry strips with melted butter and sprinkle them with parmesan cheese, Italian seasoning, and garlic salt.
- Twist the strips before placing them on a parchment-lined baking sheet.
- Bake at 400 F/ 200 C for 10-12 minutes.
- Serve and enjoy.

Per Serving: Calories: 112; Total Fat: 8g; Saturated Fat: 1.9g; Protein: 3.2g; Carbs: 7.2g; Fiber: 0.3g; Sugar: 0.2g

Cheese Garlic Breadsticks

Serves: 8 / Preparation time: 10 minutes / Cooking time: 15 minutes

2 cups all-purpose flour

1 tbsp parmesan cheese, grated

2 cups Italian cheese blend, shredded

1 tsp Italian seasoning

1 tsp garlic powder

4 tbsp butter

1 tbsp olive oil

¾ cup warm water

1 ½ tsp active dry yeast

1 tsp granulated sugar

1 ½ tsp garlic salt

- In a mixing bowl, mix together flour, yeast, sugar, and garlic salt. Slowly add warm water and mix until dough is formed.
- Knead the dough for 1-2 minutes.
- Grease separate bowl with 1 tablespoon of olive oil. Transfer dough to the greased bowl. Cover bowl and set aside for 1 hour.
- Preheat the oven to 425 F/ 218 C.
- Roll out dough on a baking sheet.
- Add butter, Italian seasoning, and garlic powder into the small microwave-safe bowl and microwave until butter is melted.
- Whisk butter mixture. Brush rolled dough with butter mixture.
- Sprinkle dough with parmesan cheese and shredded Italian cheese.
- Bake for 15-17 minutes or until cheese is melted.
- Cut bread into sticks and serve.

Per Serving: Calories: 298; Total Fat: 16.7g; Saturated Fat: 9.4g; Protein: 11g; Carbs: 25.8g; Fiber: 1.1g; Sugar: 1.3g

Easy Cheesy Breadsticks

Serves: 16 / Preparation time: 10 minutes / Cooking time: 20 minutes

1 can pizza dough

2 tbsp parmesan cheese, grated

¼ cup cheddar cheese, shredded

1 cup mozzarella cheese, shredded

2 tbsp butter, softened

- Preheat the oven to 400 F/ 200 C. Line baking sheet with parchment paper.
- Spread pizza dough on a prepared baking sheet.
- Spread butter on pizza dough. Sprinkle pizza dough with parmesan cheese, cheddar cheese, and mozzarella cheese.
- Bake in preheated oven for 15-20 minutes or until cheese is melted.
- Slice and serve.

Per Serving: Calories: 101; Total Fat: 4g; Saturated Fat: 2g; Protein: 3g; Carbs: 12g; Fiber: 0g; Sugar: 1g

Fluffy Breadsticks

Serves: 12 / Preparation time: 10 minutes / Cooking time: 12 minutes

3 cups bread flour

3 tbsp butter, melted

2 tbsp granulated sugar

1 ½ tsp Instant yeast

1 cup + 2 tbsp warm water

1 ¾ tsp kosher salt

For brushing:

¼ tsp Italian seasoning

¼ tsp garlic powder

3 tbsp butter, melted

½ tsp kosher salt

- Add warm water, yeast, sugar, butter, and salt into the stand mixer bowl and mix well. Slowly add flour and knead the dough on medium speed until smooth.
- Transfer dough to a greased bowl. Cover bowl and set aside for 1 ½ hour to rise dough.
- Divide dough into 12 pieces and roll each piece of dough into a 7-inch log.
- Place dough logs on the parchment-lined baking sheet. Cover and let rise for 1 hour.
- Preheat the oven to 400 F/ 200 C.
- Bake breadsticks for 12 minutes.
- Meanwhile, in a small bowl, mix together butter, garlic powder, Italian seasoning, and kosher salt.
- Remove breadsticks from oven and brush with melted butter mixture.
- Serve and enjoy.

Per Serving: Calories: 174; Total Fat: 6.1g; Saturated Fat: 3.7g; Protein: 3.5g; Carbs: 26.1g; Fiber: 1g; Sugar: 2.1g

Soft & Flavorful Breadsticks

Serves: 16 / Preparation time: 10 minutes / Cooking time: 15 minutes

3 ½ cups all-purpose flour

1 ½ tbsp parmesan cheese, grated

½ tsp parsley flakes

½ tsp Italian seasoning

¾ tsp garlic powder

¼ cup butter

1 tbsp olive oil

2 tbsp granulated sugar

1 tbsp active dry yeast

1 ½ cups warm water

1 tsp salt

- In a small bowl, mix warm water, sugar, and yeast until just combined. Cover and set aside for 5 minutes.
- In a large mixing bowl, add 1 cup flour and salt. Add yeast mixture and olive oil and mix well. Slowly add remaining flour and knead the dough until smooth. Cover bowl and let rise dough for 15 minutes.
- Preheat the oven to 400 F/ 200 C. Line 2 baking sheet with parchment paper.
- Place dough onto the lightly floured surface and rolled out into the rectangle. Using a pizza cutter cut into 16 pieces. Twist the ends and place breadsticks on a baking sheet.
- Add butter in microwave-safe bowl and microwave until melted. Add parmesan cheese, parsley flakes, Italian seasoning, and garlic powder in melted butter and stir well.
- Brush breadsticks with melted butter mixture.
- Bake for 12-15 minutes.
- Serve and enjoy.

Per Serving: Calories: 144; Total Fat: 4.2g; Saturated Fat: 2.1g; Protein: 3.4g; Carbs: 22.8g; Fiber: 0.9g; Sugar: 1.6g

Keto Breadsticks

Serves: 8 / Preparation time: 10 minutes / Cooking time: 15 minutes

4 eggs

1 tbsp Italian seasoning

1 tbsp butter

1 tsp garlic powder

2/3 cup coconut flour

4 tbsp cream cheese

3 cups mozzarella cheese, shredded

1 tsp sea salt

- Preheat the oven to 350 F/ 180 C.
- Add shredded mozzarella cheese into the non-stick pan and heat until cheese is fully melted.
- Once the cheese is melted then add cream cheese and butter and mix until well combined.
- Turn off the heat. Slowly add remaining ingredients and mix until well combined.
- Divide mixture into 8 equal pieces. Roll each piece and make small buns. Cover buns for 15-30 minutes.
- Roll each bun into a log and place onto a parchment-lined baking sheet.
- Bake for 15 minutes.
- Serve and enjoy.

Per Serving: Calories: 103; Total Fat: 7.9g; Saturated Fat: 4.1g; Protein: 6.4g; Carbs: 1.8g; Fiber: 0.5g; Sugar: 0.5g

Oregano Breadsticks

Serves: 16 / Preparation time: 10 minutes / Cooking time: 20 minutes

1 lb pizza dough

1 tbsp dried oregano

3 tbsp Asiago cheese, grated

1 ½ tbsp olive oil

- Preheat the oven to 400 F/ 200 C. Line 2 baking sheets with parchment paper and set aside.
- Divide dough into 16 pieces and roll each piece into a 12-inch long breadstick on a lightly floured surface.
- Place breadsticks onto the prepared baking sheets.
- Brush breadsticks with oil and sprinkle with oregano and Asiago cheese.
- Bake in preheated oven for 15-20 minutes.
- Serve and enjoy.

Per Serving: Calories: 148; Total Fat: 10.3g; Saturated Fat: 2.5g; Protein: 1.9g; Carbs: 12.2g; Fiber: 1.1g; Sugar: 0.1g

Zucchini Breadsticks

Serves: 4 / Preparation time: 10 minutes / Cooking time: 27 minutes

1 egg

1 tbsp fresh parsley, chopped

¼ cup parmesan cheese, shredded

1 tbsp butter, melted

¼ tsp ground white pepper

1 tsp Italian seasoning

¼ cup almond flour

4 oz mozzarella cheese, shredded

2 cups zucchini, shredded & squeezed out all liquid

½ tsp salt

- Preheat the oven to 420 F/ 220 C. Line baking sheet with parchment paper and set aside.
- In a mixing bowl, mix together egg, Italian seasoning, almond flour, half mozzarella cheese, zucchini, pepper, and salt.
- Spoon mixture onto the prepared cookie sheet and press into a rectangle.
- Bake for 15 minutes.
- Remove from the oven and flip carefully. Brush with butter and top with parmesan cheese and remaining mozzarella cheese.
- Bake for 8-12 minutes more or until cheese is melted.
- Garnish with parsley and cut into 12 pieces.
- Serve and enjoy.

Per Serving: Calories: 258; Total Fat: 18.4g; Saturated Fat: 9g; Protein: 19.2g; Carbs: 5.4g; Fiber: 1.4g; Sugar: 1.4g

Keto Garlic Cheese Breadsticks

Serves: 2 / Preparation time: 10 minutes / Cooking time: 15 minutes

1 egg

1 tsp garlic powder

1 cup parmesan cheese, shredded

1 cup mozzarella cheese, shredded

- Preheat the oven to 350 F/ 180 C. Line baking sheet with parchment paper and set aside.
- In a mixing bowl, add all ingredients and mix until well combined.
- Place mixture onto the prepared parchment-lined baking sheet and flatten it like pizza crust.
- Bake for 15 minutes.
- Slice and serve.

Per Serving: Calories: 242; Total Fat: 15.6g; Saturated Fat: 9.1g; Protein: 22.2g; Carbs: 3.1g; Fiber: 0.1g; Sugar: 0.5g

Cinnamon Breadsticks

Serves: 16 / Preparation time: 10 minutes / Cooking time: 20 minutes

2 ¼ cup all-purpose flour

2 tbsp brown sugar

2 tsp cinnamon

2 tbsp butter, melted

1 cup warm water

2 tsp sugar

1 tbsp olive oil

¼ oz instant yeast

¼ tsp salt

- Line baking sheet with parchment paper and set aside.
- Add flour, sugar, oil, yeast, water, and salt into the stand mixer bowl and knead for 5 minutes.
- Transfer dough onto the baking sheet and roll out the dough in a rectangular shape. Cut into the 16 pieces. Cover dough and set aside to rise for 40 minutes.
- Preheat the oven to 350 F/ 180 C.
- Brush the breadsticks with melted butter. In a small bowl mix together cinnamon and brown sugar and sprinkle over breadsticks.
- Bake breadsticks for 20 minutes.
- Serve and enjoy.

Per Serving: Calories: 92; Total Fat: 2.5g; Saturated Fat: 1.1g; Protein: 2g; Carbs: 15.4g; Fiber: 0.7g; Sugar: 1.7g

Italian Breadsticks

Serves: 16 / Preparation time: 10 minutes / Cooking time: 12 minutes

2 eggs

½ tsp dried basil

2 tsp dried parsley

1 tsp garlic salt

1 tbsp nutritional yeast

2 tsp baking powder

1 tbsp psyllium husk powder

2 garlic cloves, grated

2 tbsp parmesan cheese, grated

3 oz cream cheese

2 ½ cups mozzarella cheese, shredded

1 ½ cups almond flour

- Preheat the oven to 400 F/ 200 C.
- Add cream cheese and mozzarella cheese in microwave-safe bowl and microwave for 1 minute. Stir for 30 seconds or until cheese is melted.
- In a separate bowl, mix together almond flour, baking powder, garlic salt, parsley, oregano, basil, nutritional yeast, and psyllium husk powder.
- Add eggs and garlic in melted mozzarella cheese mixture and stir to combine.
- Add egg mixture and parmesan cheese into the flour mixture and mix until dough is formed.
- Divide dough into the 8 equal pieces. Form dough pieces logs and divide them into the 16 breadsticks.
- Place breadsticks onto the parchment-lined baking sheet and bake for 12 minutes.
- Serve and enjoy.

Per Serving: Calories: 107; Total Fat: 8.6g; Saturated Fat: 2.3g; Protein: 5.1g; Carbs: 4g; Fiber: 1.8g; Sugar: 0.5g

Taco Chicken Breadsticks

Serves: 8 / Preparation time: 10 minutes / Cooking time: 20 minutes

1 cup cooked chicken breast, shredded

½ cup sour cream

1 ½ cups cheddar cheese, shredded

12 oz pizza dough

2 ½ tsp taco seasoning

- Preheat the oven to 350 F/ 180 C. Line baking sheet with parchment paper.
- In a mixing bowl, mix together shredded chicken and 1 tsp taco seasoning.
- Place pizza dough onto the baking sheet and flatten into a rectangular shape.
- Top half dough with cheese and shredded chicken mixture. Fold half dough over filled dough.
- Sprinkle with ½ tsp taco seasoning and using a pizza cutter cut into 8 breadsticks.
- Bake for 20-25 minutes.
- In a small bowl, mix together sour cream and remaining taco seasoning.
- Serve breadsticks with sour cream.

Per Serving: Calories: 343; Total Fat: 23.7g; Saturated Fat: 9.8g; Protein: 13.2g; Carbs: 19.1g; Fiber: 1.5g; Sugar: 0.3g

Easy Pizza Dough Breadsticks

Serves: 14 / Preparation time: 10 minutes / Cooking time: 15 minutes

1 roll pizza dough

1 tbsp parsley

¼ cup parmesan cheese

1 cup mozzarella cheese, shredded

½ tsp garlic powder

2 tbsp butter, melted

- Preheat the oven to 375 F/ 180 C. Line baking sheet with parchment paper.
- Roll out pizza dough and place onto the baking sheet.
- Brush dough with melted butter and sprinkle with garlic powder.
- Top with cheeses and parsley.
- Bake in preheated oven for 12-15 minutes.
- Slice and serve.

Per Serving: Calories: 115; Total Fat: 5g; Saturated Fat: 3g; Protein: 5g; Carbs: 14g; Fiber: 1g; Sugar: 2g

Delicious Zucchini Breadsticks

Serves: 12 / Preparation time: 10 minutes / Cooking time: 30 minutes

2 zucchini, shredded

2 cups mozzarella cheese, shredded

2 eggs

1 tbsp Italian seasoning

1 tbsp garlic, minced

½ tsp salt

For topping:

1 cup mozzarella cheese, shredded

- Preheat the oven to 425 F/ 218 C.
- In a mixing bowl, mix zucchini, cheese, eggs, spices, and garlic.
- Place zucchini mixture onto the parchment-lined baking sheet and spread in a rectangular shape.
- Bake for 20-22 minutes. Top with remaining mozzarella cheese and bake for 5-7 minutes more.
- Slice and serve.

Per Serving: Calories: 40; Total Fat: 2.4g; Saturated Fat: 1.1g; Protein: 3.49g; Carbs: 1.8g; Fiber: 0.4g; Sugar: 3.4g

Easy Pesto Breadsticks

Serves: 16 / Preparation time: 10 minutes / Cooking time: 15 minutes

14 oz can pizza crust

1 cup mozzarella cheese, shredded

1 cup smoked gouda cheese, grated

½ cup pesto

- Preheat the oven to 425 F/ 218 C.
- Unroll pizza dough onto the parchment-lined baking sheet.
- Using a pizza cutter cut dough lengthwise into 12 long strips then cut those strips in half.
- Bake for 10 minutes.
- Spread pesto on baked breadsticks and top with mozzarella and gouda cheese.
- Bake for 5 minutes more.
- Serve and enjoy.

Per Serving: Calories: 109; Total Fat: 5.1g; Saturated Fat: 1.5g; Protein: 3.8g; Carbs: 12.5g; Fiber: 0.5g; Sugar: 2g

Rosemary Cheese Breadsticks

Serves: 24 / Preparation time: 10 minutes / Cooking time: 15 minutes

11 oz breadstick dough

1 tsp fresh rosemary, chopped

1/3 cup Gruyere cheese, grated

¼ cup parmesan cheese, grated

- Preheat the oven to 350 F/ 180 C. Line 2 baking sheets with parchment paper and set aside.
- In a shallow dish, mix together parmesan cheese, Gruyere cheese, and rosemary.
- Spread dough into the rectangular shape. Using a pizza cutter cut thin dough strips lengthwise.
- Coat each dough strips in cheese mixture then twist and place on the baking sheet.
- Bake breadsticks for 10-15 minutes.
- Serve and enjoy.

Per Serving: Calories: 64; Total Fat: 2.5g; Saturated Fat: 1.3g; Protein: 3.5g; Carbs: 6.5g; Fiber: 0.3g; Sugar: 0.8g

Cauliflower Breadsticks

Serves: 8 / Preparation time: 10 minutes / Cooking time: 30 minutes

6 cups cauliflower rice

½ tsp ground pepper

1 egg, lightly beaten

1 oz parmesan cheese, grated

¾ cup mozzarella cheese, shredded

1 tsp dried parsley

1 tsp dried basil

1 tsp salt

- Preheat the oven to 425 F/ 218 C. Line baking sheet with parchment paper and set aside.
- Microwave cauliflower rice for 8 minutes or until tender. Squeezed out excess liquid from cauliflower rice.
- In a mixing bowl, mix together cauliflower rice, pepper, egg, parmesan cheese, half mozzarella cheese, parsley, basil, and salt.
- Place cauliflower mixture onto the baking sheet and spread into 11*9-inch rectangle.
- Bake for 20 minutes.
- Top with remaining mozzarella cheese and bake for 10 minutes more.
- Slice and serve.

Per Serving: Calories: 46; Total Fat: 1.9g; Saturated Fat: 1g; Protein: 4.1g; Carbs: 4.3g; Fiber: 1.9g; Sugar: 1.8g

Tasty Italian Breadsticks

Serves: 8 / Preparation time: 10 minutes / Cooking time: 10 minutes

1 ¼ cup self-rising flour

¼ cup cheddar cheese, shredded

½ tsp Italian seasoning

½ tsp garlic powder

4 tbsp butter, melted

1 cup yogurt

- In a mixing bowl, add 1 cup flour and yogurt and mix until well combined.
- Transfer dough onto the flat surface and knead the dough using the remaining flour until smooth.
- Divide dough into the 8 equal pieces. Roll each dough piece and make a thin log.
- Arrange logs on the parchment-lined baking sheet.
- In a small bowl, mix together butter, garlic powder, and Italian seasonings.
- Brush breadsticks with butter mixture and sprinkle with shredded cheddar cheese.
- Bake breadsticks at 425 F/ 218 C for 10-15 minutes.
- Serve and enjoy.

Per Serving: Calories: 160; Total Fat: 7.6g; Saturated Fat: 4.7g; Protein: 4.7g; Carbs: 17.3g; Fiber: 0.6g; Sugar: 2.3g

Cheesiest Breadsticks

Serves: 10 / Preparation time: 10 minutes / Cooking time: 15 minutes

8 oz can crescent rolls

1 ½ tbsp butter, melted

1 ½ cups mozzarella cheese, grated

- Preheat the oven to 375 F/ 190 C. Line baking sheet with parchment paper and set aside.
- Unfold the crescent rolls onto the baking sheet and spread into the rectangle shape.
- Spread cheese onto half of the dough.
- Fold the other half over the cheese. Using knife cut dough into 10 strips.
- Brush dough with melted butter and bake for 13-15 minutes.
- Serve and enjoy.

Per Serving: Calories: 117; Total Fat: 7.3g; Saturated Fat: 2.8g; Protein: 2.9g; Carbs: 9.3g; Fiber: 0g; Sugar: 1.7g

Broccoli Breadsticks

Serves: 12 / Preparation time: 10 minutes / Cooking time: 35 minutes

4 cups broccoli, chopped

2 tbsp water

¼ cup fresh basil

2 eggs

1 tbsp psyllium husk

3 tbsp nutritional yeast

¼ tsp sea salt

- Preheat the oven to 375 F/ 190 C. Line baking sheet with parchment paper and set aside.
- Add broccoli into the food processor and process until it looks like rice texture.
- Add basil, psyllium husk, nutritional yeast, and sea salt and pulse until combined.
- Transfer broccoli mixture into the mixing bowl. Add water and eggs and stir to combine.
- Spread dough evenly onto the prepared baking sheet and bake for 30-35 minutes.
- Slice and serve.

Per Serving: Calories: 37; Total Fat: 1g; Saturated Fat: 0.3g; Protein: 2.9g; Carbs: 6g; Fiber: 3.8g; Sugar: 0.6g

Perfect Sour Cream Breadsticks

Serves: 12 / Preparation time: 10 minutes / Cooking time: 12 minutes

2 cups all-purpose flour

2 tbsp butter, melted

1 ¼ cups sour cream

2 tbsp fresh chives

1/3 cup butter

3 tsp baking powder

½ tsp salt

- Preheat the oven to 450 F/ 232 C.
- In a large mixing bowl, mix together flour, baking powder, and salt. Add 1/3 cup butter, sour cream, and chives and mix until well combined.
- Knead dough onto the lightly floured surface until smooth.
- Roll dough into a 12*8-inch rectangle. Cut dough into 12 1-inch wide strips.
- Place dough strips onto the parchment-lined baking sheet. Brush dough strips with melted butter.
- Bake for 10-12 minutes.
- Serve and enjoy.

Per Serving: Calories: 191; Total Fat: 12.3g; Saturated Fat: 7.6g; Protein: 3g; Carbs: 17.5g; Fiber: 0.6g; Sugar: 0.1g

Garlic Almond Flour Breadsticks

Serves: 8 / Preparation time: 10 minutes / Cooking time: 20 minutes

2 eggs

1 tsp Italian seasoning

1 tsp garlic powder

¾ cup almond flour

1 tsp baking powder

¼ cup cream cheese

3 cups mozzarella cheese, shredded

- Add almond flour, garlic powder, Italian seasoning, and baking powder in the bowl of a stand mixer. Mix well and set aside.
- Add mozzarella cheese and cream cheese in microwave-safe bowl and microwave for 1 minute. Stir until cheese is melted.
- Add eggs and melted cheese into the almond flour mixture and mix until dough forms.
- Preheat the oven to 350 F/ 180 C. Line baking sheet with parchment paper and set aside.
- Divide dough into the 8 equal pieces. Roll each dough piece into 6 inches long and make a log.
- Place all logs onto the parchment-lined baking sheet and bake for 18-20 minutes.
- Serve and enjoy.

Per Serving: Calories: 135; Total Fat: 10.9g; Saturated Fat: 3.5g; Protein: 7.2g; Carbs: 3.5g; Fiber: 1.2g; Sugar: 0.6g

Sesame Seed Breadsticks

Serves: 12 / Preparation time: 10 minutes / Cooking time: 50 minutes

1 ½ cups all-purpose flour

1/3 cup sesame seeds

2/3 cup warm water

1 tsp olive oil

¾ tsp sugar

1 tsp instant yeast

¾ tsp salt

- Line baking sheet with parchment paper and set aside.
- Spread sesame seeds on a shallow dish and set aside.
- In a mixing bowl, mix together flour, sugar, yeast, and salt. Slowly add oil and water and knead until a soft dough is form.
- Make 12 breadsticks from dough and coat with sesame seeds and place on a parchment-lined baking sheet. Cover and set aside to rise for about 1 hour.
- Preheat the oven to 325 F/ 162 C.
- Bake breadsticks for 25 minutes. Turn breadsticks and bake for 25 minutes more.
- Serve and enjoy.

Per Serving: Calories: 85; Total Fat: 2.6g; Saturated Fat: 0.4g; Protein: 2.5g; Carbs: 13.3g; Fiber: 1g; Sugar: 0.3g

Almond Coconut Flour Breadsticks

Serves: 5 / Preparation time: 10 minutes / Cooking time: 12 minutes

1 egg

3 tbsp parmesan cheese, grated

2 tbsp butter, melted

1 oz cream cheese

1 ½ cups mozzarella cheese, shredded

1 tsp onion powder

1 tsp garlic powder

1 tsp baking powder

1 ½ tsp Italian seasoning

3 tbsp coconut flour

¼ cup almond flour

½ tsp sea salt

- Preheat the oven to 400 F/ 200 C. Line baking sheet with parchment paper and set aside.
- In a small bowl, mix together almond flour, onion powder, garlic powder, baking powder, Italian seasoning, coconut flour, and salt.
- Add cream cheese and mozzarella cheese into the microwave-safe bowl and microwave for 1 minute. Stir until cheese is melted.
- Add egg and dry ingredients into the melted cheese mixture and mix everything well.
- Spread dough onto the prepared baking sheet in rectangle shape. Using a pizza cutter cut dough into the 10 breadsticks.
- Bake for 12 minutes.
- Brush breadsticks with butter and sprinkle with parmesan cheese.
- Serve and enjoy.

Per Serving: Calories: 181; Total Fat: 13.8g; Saturated Fat: 7.1g; Protein: 7.1g; Carbs: 7.9g; Fiber: 3.7g; Sugar: 1.3g

Simple Puff Pastry Breadsticks

Serves: 24 / Preparation time: 10 minutes / Cooking time: 15 minutes

2 puff pastry sheets, thawed

2 tbsp water

2 egg whites

1 tsp garlic salt

- Preheat the oven to 400 F/ 200 C. Line baking sheet with parchment paper and set aside.
- Unfold the pastry sheets and place them onto the baking sheet.
- In a bowl, whisk together egg whites, garlic salt, and water and spread over pastry sheets.
- Using a pizza cutter cut puff pastry into ¾ -inch strips.
- Bake for 15 minutes.
- Serve and enjoy.

Per Serving: Calories: 20; Total Fat: 1.3g; Saturated Fat: 0.8g; Protein: 0.6g; Carbs: 1.8g; Fiber: 0.1g; Sugar: 0.1g

Cranberry Breadsticks

Serves: 32 / Preparation time: 10 minutes / Cooking time: 15 minutes

4 cups bread flour

½ cup butter, melted

½ cup dried cranberries, chopped

1 tbsp honey

1 cup pumpkin puree

0.25 oz active dry yeast

¾ cup warm water

- In a small bowl, mix together warm water and yeast and let sit for 5 minutes.
- Add yeast mixture, honey, and pumpkin in stand mixer bowl and mix to combine. Slowly add 3 cups of bread flour.
- Add cranberries and remaining 1 cup flour and knead for 4-5 minutes or until a smooth dough is formed.
- Make 8-inch long thin breadsticks from dough and place onto the parchment-lined baking sheets. Cover and let rise for 30-60 minutes.
- Preheat the oven to 400 F/ 200 C.
- Bake breadstick for 15 minutes.
- Brush breadsticks with melted butter and serve.

Per Serving: Calories: 89; Total Fat: 3.1g; Saturated Fat: 1.9g; Protein: 1.8g; Carbs: 13.3g; Fiber: 0.8g; Sugar: 0.9g

Buttery Cinnamon Breadsticks

Serves: 48 / Preparation time: 10 minutes / Cooking time: 15 minutes

1 egg

¼ cup butter, softened

½ cup warm milk

¼ cup granulated sugar

4 ½ cups all-purpose flour

¾ cup warm water

1 ¼ oz active dry yeast

1 ½ tsp salt

For filling:

4 tsp ground cinnamon

¾ cup brown sugar

1/3 cup butter, melted

- In a mixing bowl, dissolve yeast in ¼ cup of warm water. Add milk, sugar, 2 cups of flour, egg, butter, and remaining warm water and beat on medium speed for 3-4 minutes.
- Slowly add remaining flour and mix until a soft dough is formed.
- Transfer dough onto the lightly floured surface and knead for 10 minutes or until smooth.
- Place dough in a greased bowl. Cover and let rise for 1 hour.
- Roll dough into the large rectangle and brush with butter.
- Mix together cinnamon and brown sugar and sprinkle over butter. Let dough sit for 10 minutes.
- Preheat the oven to 350 F/ 180 C.
- Cut dough into 48 strips and twist each strip and place onto the parchment-lined baking sheets. Cover and let rise for 30 minutes.
- Bake for 15 minutes.

- Serve and enjoy.

Per Serving: Calories: 80; Total Fat: 2.5g; Saturated Fat: 1.5g; Protein: 1.7g; Carbs: 12.8g; Fiber: 0.6g; Sugar: 3.4g

Amaranth Breadsticks

Serves: 14 / Preparation time: 10 minutes / Cooking time: 20 minutes

1 cup amaranth flour

1 tsp olive oil

½ tsp garlic powder

1 tsp xanthan gum

0.25 oz instant yeast

2 tbsp sugar

3 tbsp whole amaranth seeds

3 tbsp tapioca flour

1/3 cup potato starch

½ tsp salt

- Line baking sheet with parchment paper and set aside.
- In a mixing bowl, mix together amaranth flour, garlic powder, xanthan gum, yeast, sugar, amaranth seeds, tapioca flour, potato starch, and salt. Stir in ¾ cup plus 1 tablespoon of warm water and oil and mix until a smooth dough is formed.
- Make 14 thin breadsticks from dough and place onto the prepared baking sheet. Cover and let rise for 30 minutes.
- Preheat the oven to 400 F/ 200 C.
- Bake breadsticks for 20 minutes.
- Serve and enjoy.

Per Serving: Calories: 112; Total Fat: 1.3g; Saturated Fat: 0.3g; Protein: 2.2g; Carbs: 23.3g; Fiber: 1.7g; Sugar: 2g

Broccoli Cheese Breadsticks

Serves: 12 / Preparation time: 10 minutes / Cooking time: 20 minutes

2 eggs

4 cups broccoli, chopped

1 tbsp oregano

1 tsp onion powder

1 tsp garlic powder

½ cup parmesan cheese, grated

1 cup mozzarella cheese, grated

- Preheat the oven to 375 F/ 190 C. Line baking sheet with parchment paper and set aside.
- Add broccoli into the food processor and process until it looks like rice texture.
- Transfer broccoli mixture into the mixing bowl. Add remaining ingredients and stir until well combined.
- Spread broccoli mixture onto the prepared baking sheet and bake for 20 minutes.
- Slice and serve.

Per Serving: Calories: 80; Total Fat: 4.3g; Saturated Fat: 2.5g; Protein: 6.6g; Carbs: 2.7g; Fiber: 1g; Sugar: 0.7g

BUNS

Whole Wheat Buns

Serves: 12 / Preparation time: 10 minutes / Cooking time: 20 minutes

1 egg white, lightly beaten

4 cups whole wheat flour

1 egg, lightly beaten

2 tbsp honey

¼ cup vegetable oil

½ cup warm milk

1 cup warm water

2 ¼ tsp active dry yeast

1 ½ tsp salt

- Add warm water and yeast in stand mixer bowl. Stir well and let sit for 5 minutes. Stir in egg, honey, oil, milk, and salt until combined.
- Add 4 cups flour and mix on medium speed until the dough is formed.
- Transfer dough onto the floured surface and knead until smooth.
- Place dough into the greased bowl. Cover and let rise for 1 ½ hour.
- Punch down risen dough and divide 12 equal pieces. Shape each dough piece into a bun shape and place onto the parchment-lined baking sheets. Cover buns and let rise for 20 minutes.
- Gently flatten each bun. Cover again and let rise for 30 minutes more.
- Brush buns with beaten egg whites and sprinkle with sesame seeds.
- Bake at 375 F/ 190 C for 18-20 minutes.
- Let it cool completely then serve.

Per Serving: Calories: 226; Total Fat: 5.6g; Saturated Fat: 1.2g; Protein: 6g; Carbs: 37.5g; Fiber: 1.4g; Sugar: 3.5g

Perfect Hamburger Buns

Serves: 12 / Preparation time: 10 minutes / Cooking time: 10 minutes

1 egg

4 cups flour

¼ cup sugar

1/3 cup vegetable oil

1 cup warm water

2 tsp active dry yeast

1 tsp salt

- Add warm water and yeast into the mixing bowl and mix well. Cover and set aside for 5-10 minutes.
- Add egg, sugar, oil, and salt into the yeast mixture and stir until combined.
- Slowly add flour and mix until dough is formed.
- Transfer dough onto the floured surface and knead until smooth.
- Divide dough into the 12 equal pieces. Shape each dough piece into a bun shape and place onto the parchment-lined baking sheet. Cover buns and let rise for 10 minutes.
- Preheat the oven to 425 F/ 218 C.
- Bake buns for 10-12 minutes.
- Serve and enjoy.

Per Serving: Calories: 228; Total Fat: 6.9g; Saturated Fat: 1.4g; Protein: 5g; Carbs: 36.3g; Fiber: 1.3g; Sugar: 4.3g

Tasty Hamburger Buns

Serves: 12 / Preparation time: 10 minutes / Cooking time: 15 minutes

5 cups all-purpose flour

¼ cup sugar

½ cup vegetable oil

¾ cup water

1 cup milk

0.25 oz dry yeast

1 tsp salt

- In a mixing bowl, mix together 2 cups flour and yeast.
- In a separate bowl, add milk, sugar, water, oil, and salt, and microwave until lukewarm.
- Add flour mixture into the milk mixture and mix until smooth, about 3 minutes.
- Add remaining flour and mix until a soft dough is formed.
- Transfer dough onto the floured surface and knead for 10 minutes. Place dough in a greased bowl and let sit for 10 minutes.
- Divide dough into the 12 equal pieces. Shape each dough piece into a bun shape and place onto the parchment-lined baking sheet. Cover buns and let rise for 30 minutes.
- Bake at 400 F/ 200 C for 12-15 minutes.
- Serve and enjoy.

Per Serving: Calories: 297; Total Fat: 10g; Saturated Fat: 2.1g; Protein: 6.3g; Carbs: 45.1g; Fiber: 1.5g; Sugar: 5.2g

Soft Burger Buns

Serves: 8 / Preparation time: 10 minutes / Cooking time: 15 minutes

1 cup warm water

1 tbsp instant yeast

¼ cup sugar

3 ½ cups all-purpose flour

1 egg

2 tbsp butter, melted

1 ¼ tsp salt

- Add flour, egg, sugar, yeast, and salt into the mixing bowl and mix well. Slowly add warm water and knead the dough using a hand mixer until smooth and soft.
- Transfer dough into the greased bowl. Cover dough and let rise for 1-2 hours.
- Punch down the dough. Divide dough into the 8 equal pieces. Shape each dough piece into a bun shape and place onto the parchment-lined baking sheet. Cover buns and let rise for 60 minutes.
- Brush buns with half melted butter and bake at 375 F/ 190 C for 15-18 minutes.
- Brush buns with remaining melted butter.
- Serve and enjoy.

Per Serving: Calories: 260; Total Fat: 4g; Saturated Fat: 2.1g; Protein: 6.9g; Carbs: 48.6g; Fiber: 1.8g; Sugar: 6.4g

Fluffy Raisin Buns

Serves: 8 / Preparation time: 10 minutes / Cooking time: 20 minutes

2 cups flour

2 ½ tsp dry yeast

2/3 cup raisins

3 tbsp butter, melted

1 egg

1/3 cup warm milk

2 tbsp sugar

½ tsp salt

- In a small bowl, mix together warm milk, yeast, and 1 tablespoon sugar and let sit for 5 minutes.
- In a large bowl, mix together flour, egg, remaining sugar, and salt. Add yeast mixture and melted butter and knead the dough until smooth.
- Transfer dough into the greased bowl. Cover and let rise for 1 hour.
- Punch down the dough and transfer onto the floured surface. Add raisins and mix well in the dough.
- Divide dough into the 8 equal pieces. Shape each dough piece into a bun shape and place onto the parchment-lined baking sheet. Cover buns and let rise for 30 minutes.
- Preheat the oven to 350 F/ 180 C.
- Bake buns for 20 minutes.
- Serve and enjoy.

Per Serving: Calories: 216; Total Fat: 5.5g; Saturated Fat: 3.1g; Protein: 5.2g; Carbs: 37.4g; Fiber: 1.6g; Sugar: 10.7g

Keto Buns

Serves: 6 / Preparation time: 10 minutes / Cooking time: 26 minutes

4 eggs

1 tsp onion flakes

1 tbsp black sesame seeds

1 tbsp white sesame seeds

1 tbsp rosemary

¾ cup almond flour

4 tbsp butter, melted

½ tsp Himalayan salt

- Preheat the oven to 430 F/ 220 C.
- Add all ingredients into the blender and blend until well mixed.
- Pour blended mixture into 6 silicone jumbo muffin molds and bake for 26 minutes.
- Serve and enjoy.

Per Serving: Calories: 207; Total Fat: 18.9g; Saturated Fat: 6.4g; Protein: 7.3g; Carbs: 4.3g; Fiber: 1.9g; Sugar: 0.8g

Almond Flour Buns

Serves: 6 / Preparation time: 10 minutes / Cooking time: 60 minutes

3 egg whites

1 cup boiling water

1 tsp white wine vinegar

1 tsp baking powder

1 tbsp monk fruit sweetener

5 tbsp psyllium husk whole

¾ cup almond flour

¾ tsp sea salt

- Preheat the oven to 350 F/ 180 C.
- In a mixing bowl, mix together almond flour, sweetener, baking powder, psyllium husk, and salt.
- Add boiling water, vinegar, and egg whites and stir for 3-5 minutes.
- Divide dough into 6 equal portions. Place 6 dough mounds onto the parchment-lined baking sheet and bake for 50-60 minutes.
- Allow to cool completely then serve.

Per Serving: Calories: 160; Total Fat: 7g; Saturated Fat: 0.5g; Protein: 4.8g; Carbs: 31.7g; Fiber: 25g; Sugar: 0.6g

Jalapeno Wheat Buns

Serves: 8 / Preparation time: 10 minutes / Cooking time: 30 minutes

1 egg, lightly beaten

3 jalapeno peppers, chopped

5 oz cheddar cheese, shredded

1 cup all-purpose flour

2 ½ tbsp sugar

¼ cup potato flour

2 tbsp olive oil

1 ¼ cups warm water

2 ¼ tsp instant yeast

2 cups whole wheat flour

1 tsp salt

- Line baking sheet with parchment paper and set aside.
- Add flours, yeast, oil, sugar, salt, potato flour, and water into the stand mixer bowl and mix on medium speed until a soft dough is form.
- Add peppers and cheese and mix on medium-low speed for 5 minutes.
- Transfer dough in a greased bowl. Cover and let rise for 1 ½ hour.
- Divide dough into the 8 equal pieces. Shape each dough piece into a bun shape and place onto the parchment-lined baking sheet. Cover buns and let rise for 30 minutes.
- Preheat the oven to 350 F/ 180 C.
- In a small bowl, whisk the egg with 1 tablespoon of water.
- Brush buns with egg wash and bake for 20-30 minutes.

Per Serving: Calories: 269; Total Fat: 10.7g; Saturated Fat: 4.5g; Protein:

10.1g; Carbs: 33.9g; Fiber: 3.2g; Sugar: 4.3g

PRETZELS, MUFFINS, CAKES, BAGUETTE, & SNACKS

Soft Pretzels

Serves: 12 / Preparation time: 10 minutes / Cooking time: 8 minutes

5 cups all-purpose flour

4 cup hot water

½ cup baking soda

1 tbsp vegetable oil

½ cup white sugar

1 ¼ cups warm water

1 tsp white sugar

4 tsp active dry yeast

1 ½ tsp salt

- In a small bowl, add yeast, warm water, and 1 tsp sugar and stir until yeast is dissolved. Cover and let sit for 10 minutes.
- In a large mixing bowl, mix together flour, ½ cup sugar, and salt. Add yeast mixture and oil and mix until dough is formed. Knead the dough for 8-10 minutes.
- Transfer dough into the greased bowl. Cover and let rise for 1 hour.
- Preheat the oven to 450 F/ 230 C. Line 2 baking sheet with parchment paper.
- In a large bowl, dissolve baking soda in hot water and set aside.
- Divide dough into 12 equal pieces. Roll each dough piece into a rope and twist into a pretzel shape.
- Dip each pretzel into the baking soda and hot water mixture and place onto the prepared baking sheets.
- Bake pretzel for 8 minutes.
- Serve and enjoy.

Per Serving: Calories: 236; Total Fat: 1.7g; Saturated Fat: 0.3g; Protein: 5.9g; Carbs: 48.9g; Fiber: 1.7g; Sugar: 8.8g

French Baguette

Serves: 20 / Preparation time: 10 minutes / Cooking time: 25 minutes

1 tbsp sugar

4 cups flour

1 1/2 cups water

1 tbsp olive oil

1/2 tsp yeast

1 1/2 tsp salt

- In a large bowl, mix together water, yeast, sugar, and salt.
- Add flour and mix until a shaggy dough is formed.
- Place dough into the greased bowl. Cover bowl and set aside for 2 hours.
- Punch down the dough and transfer onto the lightly floured surface.
- Divide dough into the two portions.
- Flatten both the dough pieces and roll them tightly and place on a greased baking sheet.
- Cover loaves with a tea towel and set aside for 30 minutes.
- Preheat the oven 400 F/ 200 C.
- Uncover the loaves and using a knife to make 3-4 cuts on top of loaves.
- Bake for 20-25 minutes.
- Slice and serve.

Per Serving: Calories: 100; Total Fat: 1g; Saturated Fat: 0.1g; Protein: 2.6g; Carbs: 19.7g; Fiber: 0.7g; Sugar: 0.7g

Coconut Flour Baguette

Serves: 12 / Preparation time: 10 minutes / Cooking time: 55 minutes

4 eggs

2 egg whites

1/3 cup coconut milk

2 tbsp coconut oil, melted

1/2 tsp baking soda

1/2 tsp apple cider vinegar

1/3 cup Psyllium husk powder

1/4 cup coconut flour

1/2 tsp salt

- Preheat the oven to 350 F/ 180 C. Line baking sheet with parchment paper and set aside.
- In a large bowl, whisk together coconut oil, coconut milk, egg whites, and eggs.
- Stir in the coconut flour and psyllium husk powder. Stir in vinegar, baking soda, and salt.
- Once the dough is ready then shape into a long loaf and place on a baking sheet.
- Bake for 50-55 minutes.
- Slices and serve.

Per Serving: Calories: 73; Total Fat: 5.4g; Saturated Fat: 3.9g; Protein: 2.6g; Carbs: 4.3g; Fiber: 3.4g; Sugar: 0.4g

Carrot Muffins

Serves: 6 / Preparation time: 10 minutes / Cooking time: 20 minutes

1 egg

1 cup all-purpose flour

1/2 tbsp canola oil

1 1/2 tsp baking powder

1/4 tsp nutmeg

1 tsp cinnamon

1/4 cup applesauce

3/4 cup grated carrots

1 tsp vanilla

1/4 cup light brown sugar

1/4 cup granulated sugar

1/4 tsp salt

- Preheat the oven to 350 F/ 180 C.
- Line muffin tray with cupcake liners and set aside.
- Add all ingredients into the bowl and mix until well combined.
- Pour batter into a prepared muffin tray.
- Bake for 20 minutes
- Serve and enjoy.

Per Serving: Calories: 165; Total Fat: 2.2g; Saturated Fat: 0.4g; Protein: 3.2g; Carbs: 33.7g; Fiber: 1.3g; Sugar: 16.2g

Lemon Muffins

Serves: 6 / Preparation time: 10 minutes / Cooking time: 15 minutes

1 egg

1 cup flour

1/2 tsp vanilla

1/2 cup milk

2 tbsp canola oil

1/4 tsp baking soda

1 tsp lemon zest, grated

1/2 cup sugar

3/4 tsp baking powder

1/2 tsp salt

- Preheat the oven to 350 F/ 180 C.
- Line muffin tray with cupcake liners and set aside.
- In a bowl, whisk egg, vanilla, milk, oil, and sugar until creamy.
- Add remaining ingredients and stir until just combined.
- Pour batter into the prepared muffin tray.
- Bake for 15 minutes.
- Serve and enjoy.

Per Serving: Calories: 202; Total Fat: 6g; Saturated Fat: 0.9g; Protein: 3.8g; Carbs: 34g; Fiber: 0.6g; Sugar: 17.8g

Delicious Carrot Cake

Serves: 4 / Preparation time: 10 minutes / Cooking time: 25 minutes

1 egg

1/2 cup flour

1/4 cup grated carrot

1/4 cup canola oil

1/4 cup walnuts, chopped

1/2 tsp baking powder

1/2 tsp vanilla

1/2 tsp cinnamon

1/2 cup sugar

- Preheat the oven to 350 F/ 180 C.
- Grease 6-inch baking dish and set aside.
- In a mixing bowl, beat sugar and oil for 1 minute. Add vanilla, cinnamon, and egg and beat for 30 seconds.
- Add remaining ingredients and stir until just combined.
- Pour batter into the prepared baking dish.
- Bake for 25 minutes.
- Serve and enjoy.

Per Serving: Calories: 341; Total Fat: 19.5g; Saturated Fat: 1.6g; Protein: 4.9g; Carbs: 39.1g; Fiber: 1.3g; Sugar: 25.6g

Raspberry Muffins

Serves: 6 / Preparation time: 10 minutes / Cooking time: 35 minutes

2 eggs

3.5 oz raspberries

5 oz almond meal

2 tbsp coconut oil

1 tsp baking powder

2 tbsp honey

- Preheat the oven to 350 F/ 180 C.
- Line muffin tray with cupcake liners and set aside.
- In a medium bowl, mix together almond meal and baking powder.
- Add honey, eggs, and oil and stir until just combined.
- Add raspberries and fold well.
- Spoon batter into a prepared muffin tray and bake for 35 minutes.
- Serve and enjoy.

Per Serving: Calories: 227; Total Fat: 17.9g; Saturated Fat: 5.3g; Protein: 7.1g; Carbs: 13.3g; Fiber: 4.1g; Sugar: 7.6g

Delicious Mini Chocolate Cake

Serves: 4 / Preparation time: 10 minutes / Cooking time: 30 minutes

1 egg

5 tbsp cocoa powder

1/2 cup all-purpose flour

1/2 tsp baking soda

1 tbsp warm coffee

1/2 tsp vanilla

1/3 cup sour cream

1/2 cup granulated sugar

1/3 cup canola oil

- Preheat the oven to 350 F/ 180 C.
- Grease 6-inch baking dish and set aside.
- In a mixing bowl, mix together flour, baking soda, and cocoa powder and set aside.
- In a small bowl, whisk together egg, vanilla, coffee, sour cream, sugar, and oil.
- Pour egg mixture into the flour mixture and mix until just combined.
- Pour batter into the prepared baking dish and bake for 30 minutes.
- Serve and enjoy.

Per Serving: Calories: 385; Total Fat: 24.3g; Saturated Fat: 4.7g; Protein: 4.8g; Carbs: 41.6g; Fiber: 2.4g; Sugar: 25.3g

Apple Cinnamon Cake

Serves: 12 / Preparation time: 10 minutes / Cooking time: 45 minutes

3 cups all-purpose flour

3 tsp baking powder

1 1/2 tbsp ground cinnamon

2 cups apples, peeled and chopped

1/4 cup sugar

1/4 cup butter, melted

12 oz apple juice

1 tsp Salt

- Preheat the oven to 350 F/ 180 C.
- Grease 8-inch baking dish and set aside.
- In a large bowl, mix together flour, salt, sugar, cinnamon, and baking powder.
- Add melted butter and apple juice and mix until well combined. Add apples and fold well.
- Pour batter into the prepared baking dish and bake for 45 minutes.
- Serve and enjoy.

Per Serving: Calories: 299; Total Fat: 4.5g; Saturated Fat: 2.6g; Protein: 3.6g; Carbs: 62.4g; Fiber: 2.7g; Sugar: 32.1g

Cranberry Muffins

Serves: 6 / Preparation time: 10 minutes / Cooking time: 30 minutes

2 eggs

1/2 cup cranberries

1 tsp vanilla

1/4 cup sour cream

1/4 tsp cinnamon

1 tsp baking powder

1/4 cup Swerve

1 1/2 cups almond flour

Pinch of salt

- Preheat the oven to 325 F/ 162 C.
- Line muffin tray with cupcake liners and set aside.
- In a bowl, beat sour cream, vanilla, and eggs.
- Add remaining ingredients except for cranberries and beat until smooth.
- Add cranberries and fold well.
- Pour batter into the prepared muffin pan and bake for 30 minutes.
- Serve and enjoy.

Per Serving: Calories: 210; Total Fat: 17.5g; Saturated Fat: 2.7g; Protein: 8.2g; Carbs: 8g; Fiber: 3.4g; Sugar: 1.5g

Simple Butter Cake

Serves: 8 / Preparation time: 10 minutes / Cooking time: 30 minutes

1 egg, beaten

1/2 cup butter, softened

1/2 tsp vanilla

1 cup all-purpose flour

3/4 cup sugar

- Preheat the oven to 350 F/ 180 C.
- Grease 8*inch baking dish and set aside.
- In a mixing bowl, mix together sugar and butter.
- Add egg, flour, and vanilla and mix until combined.
- Pour batter into the prepared baking dish and bake for 30 minutes.
- Slice and serve.

Per Serving: Calories: 238; Total Fat: 12.2g; Saturated Fat: 7.5g; Protein: 2.4g; Carbs: 30.8g; Fiber: 0.4g; Sugar: 18.9g

Ricotta Strawberry Cake

Serves: 10 / Preparation time: 10 minutes / Cooking time: 60 minutes

¾ cup heavy cream

1 box strawberry cake mix

½ cup vegetable oil

2 tsp vanilla

4 eggs

15 oz ricotta cheese

For glaze:

4 tbsp milk

1 tsp vanilla

2 cups powdered sugar

- Preheat the oven to 325 F/ 162 C. Grease 10-inch springform pan and set aside.
- In a large bowl, beat together eggs, oil, vanilla, and ricotta until well combined.
- Add cake mix and beat until just combined.
- Slowly add heavy cream and blend well.
- Pour batter in prepared pan and bake for 60 minutes.
- Remove cake from oven and allow to cool for 10 minutes.
- Meanwhile, for glaze in a mixing bowl, whisk together sugar, milk, and vanilla.
- Pour glaze over cake.
- Slice and serve.

Per Serving: Calories: 540; Total Fat: 29g; Saturated Fat: 19g; Protein: 9g; Carbs: 61g; Fiber: 0g; Sugar: 45g

Cinnamon Cake

Serves: 12 / Preparation time: 10 minutes / Cooking time: 40 minutes

3 eggs

2/3 cup milk

2 tsp vanilla

2/3 cup butter, softened

1 1/3 cup granulated sugar

1 tbsp cinnamon

1 tbsp baking powder

2 cups all-purpose flour

¾ tsp salt

- Preheat the oven to 350 F/ 180 C. Grease 10-inch cake pan and set aside.
- In a mixing bowl, mix together flour, cinnamon, baking powder, and salt.
- In a large bowl, beat together sugar, vanilla, and butter until smooth. Add eggs and beat until well combined.
- Add flour mixture and milk and mix until well combined.
- Pour batter in prepared pan and bake for 40-45 minutes.
- Remove cake from oven and allow to cool for 20 minutes.
- Slice and serve.

Per Serving: Calories: 277; Total Fat: 11.8g; Saturated Fat: 7g; Protein: 4.1g; Carbs: 40g; Fiber: 0.9g; Sugar: 23.1g

Moist Rhubarb Muffins

Serves: 12 / Preparation time: 10 minutes / Cooking time: 20 minutes

1 egg, lightly beaten

1 tsp vanilla

¼ cup canola oil

¾ cup milk

2 tsp baking powder

½ cup sugar

1 ¾ cup all-purpose flour

1 cup rhubarb

¼ tsp salt

- Preheat the oven to 400 F/ 200 C. Line muffin tray with cupcake liners and set aside.
- In a bowl, toss rhubarb with 1 tablespoon of flour and set aside.
- In a large bowl, mix together flour, baking powder, sugar, and salt.
- In a small bowl, whisk egg with oil, vanilla, and milk.
- Add egg mixture into the flour mixture and stir until well combined.
- Add rhubarb and fold well.
- Pour batter into the prepared muffin tray and bake for 18-20 minutes.
- Serve and enjoy.

Per Serving: Calories: 155; Total Fat: 5.4g; Saturated Fat: 0.7g; Protein: 2.9g; Carbs: 23.9g; Fiber: 0.7g; Sugar: 9.3g

Banana Strawberry Muffins

Serves: 12 / Preparation time: 10 minutes / Cooking time: 20 minutes

1 ½ cups fresh strawberries, chopped

1 tsp vanilla

½ cup yogurt

1/3 cup honey

½ cup coconut oil, melted

2 eggs

2 ripe bananas

1 tsp cinnamon

1 tsp baking soda

1 tsp baking powder

¼ tsp salt

- Preheat the oven to 350 F/ 180 C. Line muffin tray with cupcake liners and set aside.
- In a small bowl, mix together flour, cinnamon, baking soda, baking powder, and salt.
- In a large mixing bowl, mash bananas until smooth. Add eggs, vanilla, yogurt, honey, and coconut oil and whisk until combined.
- Add strawberries and fold well.
- Pour batter into the prepared muffin tray and bake for 18-20 minutes.
- Serve and enjoy.

Per Serving: Calories: 150; Total Fat: 10g; Saturated Fat: 8.2g; Protein: 1.9g; Carbs: 14.8g; Fiber: 1g; Sugar: 11.9g

Banana Bread Muffins

Serves: 12 / Preparation time: 10 minutes / Cooking time: 20 minutes

2 eggs, lightly beaten

1 tsp vanilla

¾ cup brown sugar

½ cup butter, melted

3 ripe bananas

½ tsp baking powder

1 tsp baking soda

1 ½ cups all-purpose flour

½ tsp salt

- Preheat the oven to 400 F/ 200 C. Line muffin tray with cupcake liners and set aside.
- In a large mixing bowl, mash bananas. Add brown sugar and melted butter and stir until well combined. Stir in vanilla and eggs until well combined.
- In a separate bowl, mix together flour, baking powder, baking soda, and salt.
- Add flour mixture into the banana mixture and mix until well combined.
- Pour batter into the prepared muffin tray and bake at 350 F/ 180 C for 20 minutes.
- Serve and enjoy.

Per Serving: Calories: 197; Total Fat: 8.7g; Saturated Fat: 5.1g; Protein: 2.9g; Carbs: 27.8g; Fiber: 1.2g; Sugar: 12.6g

Blueberry Sour Cream Muffins

Serves: 24 / Preparation time: 10 minutes / Cooking time: 20 minutes

4 eggs

2 cups sour cream

1 tsp baking soda

4 cups flour

1 tsp vanilla

1 cup canola oil

3 cups fresh blueberries

1/8 tsp nutmeg

1 ½ tsp cinnamon

1 ¼ cups brown sugar

1 ¼ cup white sugar

1 tsp salt

- Preheat the oven to 400 F/ 200 C. Line muffin tray with cupcake liners and set aside.
- In a large bowl, whisk eggs, sour cream, vanilla, oil, and sugar until well incorporated.
- In a separate bowl, mix together flour, baking soda, nutmeg, cinnamon, and salt.
- Add half of the flour mixture into the egg mixture and stir well. Add remaining flour mixture and stir until well combined.
- Add blueberries into the batter and fold well.
- Pour batter into the prepared muffin tray and bake for 20 minutes.
- Serve and enjoy.

Per Serving: Calories: 287; Total Fat: 14.1g; Saturated Fat: 3.4g; Protein: 3.8g; Carbs: 37.4g; Fiber: 1.1g; Sugar: 19.7g

Banana Cake

Serves: 8 / Preparation time: 10 minutes / Cooking time: 40 minutes

2 large eggs, beaten

2 bananas, mashed

1 tsp baking soda

2 cups all-purpose flour

1 tsp baking powder

1 1/2 cup sugar, granulated

1 tsp vanilla

1/2 cup butter

1 cup milk

- Grease baking dish and set aside.
- In a large bowl, beat together sugar and butter until creamy.
- Add beaten eggs and mix well.
- Add milk, vanilla extract, baking soda, baking powder, flour, and mashed bananas into the mixture and beat for 2-3 minutes.
- Pour batter into the prepared baking dish and bake at 350 F for 40 minutes.
- Slices and serve.

Per Serving: Calories: 418; Total Fat: 13.8g; Saturated Fat: 8.1g; Protein: 6.2g; Carbs: 70.1g; Fiber: 1.6g; Sugar: 42.7g

Chocolate Chip Cake

Serves: 10 / Preparation time: 10 minutes / Cooking time: 45 minutes

2 eggs

1 cup sugar

1 cup vegetable shortening

2 tbsp cocoa powder, unsweetened

1 tsp baking soda

1 3/4 cups flour

3/4 cup chocolate chips

1 cup boiling water

1 tsp vanilla

1 tsp salt

- Preheat the oven at 350 F. Grease baking dish and set aside.
- In a large bowl, mix together flour, cocoa powder, salt, and baking soda. Set aside.
- In a separate bowl, beat together sugar and shortening until creamy.
- Add egg and vanilla and beat for 2 minutes.
- Add flour mixture into the shortening mixture and fold well.
- Pour boiling water into the batter and mix until combine.
- Add chocolate chips into the batter and fold well.
- Pour batter into the prepared baking dish and bake for 45 minutes.
- Slice and serve.

Per Serving: Calories: 419; Total Fat: 25.5g; Saturated Fat: 9.2g; Protein: 4.5g; Carbs: 44.9g; Fiber: 1.3g; Sugar: 26.7g

Delicious Chocolate Cake

Serves: 8 / Preparation time: 10 minutes / Cooking time: 30 minutes

2 large eggs

2 3/4 cups flour

1 cup buttermilk

1 cup shortening

1 cup sugar, granulated

1 cup brown sugar

1/2 cup cocoa powder

1 tsp baking soda

1/2 cup warm water

- Grease baking dish and set aside.
- In a large bowl, beat together brown sugar, granulated sugar, and shortening until creamy.
- Add eggs, cocoa powder, flour, and buttermilk and stir to combine.
- Dissolve soda in warm water and stir into batter.
- Pour batter into the prepared baking dish and bake at 350 F for 30 minutes.
- Slice and serve.

Per Serving: Calories: 588; Total Fat: 28.3g; Saturated Fat: 8.9g; Protein: 8g; Carbs: 80.1g; Fiber: 2.8g; Sugar: 44.4g

Chocolate Muffins

Serves: 9 / Preparation time: 10 minutes / Cooking time: 25 minutes

1 egg

1/2 cup milk

1/2 cup brown sugar

1/2 cup granulated sugar

2 tbsp cocoa powder

1/2 tsp baking soda

2 tsp baking powder

1/2 cup chocolate chips

1/4 cup olive oil

1/2 cup brewed coffee

- Preheat the oven to 350 F/ 180 C.
- In a bowl, mix together flour, cocoa powder, baking soda, and baking powder.
- In a large bowl, whisk egg, vanilla, milk, oil, brown sugar, coffee, and sugar until smooth.
- Add flour mixture and chocolate chips into the egg mixture and fold well.
- Pour batter into the 9 silicone muffin molds and bake for 25 minutes.
- Serve and enjoy.

Per Serving: Calories: 188; Total Fat: 9.3g; Saturated Fat: 3.2g; Protein: 2g; Carbs: 26.5g; Fiber: 0.7g; Sugar: 24.4g

Delicious Blueberry Cake

Serves: 8 / Preparation time: 10 minutes / Cooking time: 45 minutes

1 egg

2 cups blueberries

1/2 cup butter, melted

2 cups all-purpose flour

1/2 cup milk

2 tsp baking powder

1/3 cup sugar

Pinch of salt

- Preheat the oven to 350 F/ 180 C.
- Grease 8-inch baking dish and set aside.
- In a large bowl, mix together all-purpose flour, baking powder, sugar, and salt.
- In a separate bowl, whisk egg, butter, and milk.
- Add flour mixture into the egg mixture and mix until just combined.
- Pour batter into the prepared baking dish. Add blueberries and fold well.
- Bake for 45 minutes.
- Serve and enjoy.

Per Serving: Calories: 284; Total Fat: 12.8g; Saturated Fat: 7.7g; Protein: 4.8g; Carbs: 38.8g; Fiber: 1.8g; Sugar: 12.8g

Pound Cake

Serves: 10 / Preparation time: 10 minutes / Cooking time: 55 minutes

4 eggs

1/4 cup cream cheese

1/4 cup butter

1 tsp baking powder

1 tbsp coconut flour

1 cup almond flour

1/2 cup sour cream

1 tsp vanilla

1 cup monk fruit sweetener

- Preheat the oven to 350 F. Grease 9-inch cake pan and set aside.
- In a large bowl, mix together almond flour, baking powder, and coconut flour.
- In a separate bowl, add cream cheese and butter and microwave for 30 seconds. Stir well and microwave for 30 seconds more.
- Add sour cream, vanilla, and sweetener and mix until just combined.
- Pour cream cheese mixture into the almond flour mixture and stir to combine.
- Add eggs in batter one by one and stir until just combined.
- Pour batter into the prepared cake pan and bake for 55 minutes.
- Slice and serve.

Per Serving: Calories: 182; Total Fat: 16.6g; Saturated Fat: 6.8g; Protein: 5.7g; Carbs: 4.3g; Fiber: 1.7g; Sugar: 0.7g

Peanut Butter Cake

Serves: 8 / Preparation time: 10 minutes / Cooking time: 30 minutes

1/2 cup peanut butter powder

1 1/2 cups all-purpose flour

1 cup of water

1/3 cup vegetable oil

1 tsp baking soda

1 cup of sugar

1 tsp vanilla

1 tbsp apple cider vinegar

1/2 tsp salt

- Preheat the oven to 350 F/ 180 C. Grease cake pan and set aside.
- In a mixing bowl, mix together flour, baking soda, peanut butter powder, sugar, and salt.
- In a small bowl, whisk together oil, vanilla, vinegar, and water.
- Pour oil mixture into the flour mixture and stir to combine.
- Pour batter into the prepared pan and bake for 30 minutes.
- Slice and enjoy.

Per Serving: Calories: 315; Total Fat: 11.3g; Saturated Fat: 2.1g; Protein: 10.4g; Carbs: 46g; Fiber: 2.7g; Sugar: 25.1g

Moist French Cake

Serves: 12 / Preparation time: 10 minutes / Cooking time: 35 minutes

2 eggs

7 oz all-purpose flour

2 tsp baking powder

4 tbsp olive oil

7 oz sugar

8.5 oz yogurt

- Preheat the oven to 350 F/ 180 C.
- In a large bowl, add yogurt, oil, eggs, sugar, flour, and baking powder and mix until smooth.
- Pour batter into the greased cake pan and bake for 35 minutes.
- Slice and serve.

Per Serving: Calories: 188; Total Fat: 5.8g; Saturated Fat: 1.1g; Protein: 3.8g; Carbs: 31g; Fiber: 0.5g; Sugar: 18.1g

Chocó Peanut Butter Muffins

Serves: 12 / Preparation time: 10 minutes / Cooking time: 20 minutes

1 cup peanut butter

1 cup applesauce

1/2 cup maple syrup

1/2 cup cocoa powder

1 tsp baking soda

1 tsp vanilla

- Preheat the oven to 350 F/ 180 C.
- Add all ingredients into the blender and blend until smooth.
- Pour blended mixture into the 12 silicone muffin molds and bake for 20 minutes.
- Serve and enjoy.

Per Serving: Calories: 178; Total Fat: 11.3g; Saturated Fat: 2.6g; Protein: 6.1g; Carbs: 17.3g; Fiber: 2.6g; Sugar: 12g

Chocó Chip Pumpkin Muffins

Serves: 12 / Preparation time: 10 minutes / Cooking time: 35 minutes

2 eggs

2 cups all-purpose flour

1/2 cup chocolate chips

1 tsp baking soda

1 cup can pumpkin

1/2 cup olive oil

1/2 cup maple syrup

1 tsp pumpkin pie spice

1/2 tsp salt

- Preheat the oven to 350 F/ 180 C.
- Line muffin tray with cupcake liners and set aside.
- In a large bowl, mix together flour, pumpkin pie spice, baking soda, and salt.
- In a separate bowl, whisk together eggs, pumpkin puree, oil, and maple syrup.
- Slowly add flour mixture to the wet mixture and mix well.
- Add chocolate chips and fold well.
- Pour batter into the prepared muffin tray and bake for 35 minutes.
- Serve and enjoy.

Per Serving: Calories: 237; Total Fat: 11.5g; Saturated Fat: 3g; Protein: 3.8g; Carbs: 30.7g; Fiber: 1.4g; Sugar: 12.2g

Easy Baked Donuts

Serves: 12 / Preparation time: 10 minutes / Cooking time: 15 minutes

2 eggs

1 cup all-purpose flour

1/2 tsp vanilla

1 tsp baking powder

3/4 cup sugar

1/2 cup buttermilk

1/4 cup vegetable oil

1/2 tsp salt

- Preheat the oven to 350 F/ 180 C.
- Grease donut pan and set aside.
- In a bowl, mix together oil, vanilla, baking powder, sugar, eggs, buttermilk, and salt until well combined.
- Add flour and stir to combine.
- Pour batter into the prepared donut pan and bake for 15 minutes.
- Serve and enjoy.

Per Serving: Calories: 140; Total Fat: 5.5g; Saturated Fat: 1.2g; Protein: 2.3g; Carbs: 21.2g; Fiber: 0.3g; Sugar: 13.1g

<u>The Fresh Loaf (thefreshloaf.com)</u>

This online community for amateur artisan bakers includes recipes, reviews, lessons, and more.

<u>Maurizio Leo (@maurizio)</u>

Leo is a Saveur blog award-winner (his blog is The Perfect Loaf), so his Instagram is a great follow for any aspiring baker. His feed is full of all kinds of bread, including baguettes, bagels, and more. He has a special focus on naturally-leavened sourdough. His website link is in his bio.

Breadtopia (breadtopia.com)

Founder Eric has built a great community for breadmakers. His blog includes video walkthroughs, product reviews, recipes for homemade artisanal bread, as well as muffins, cookies, and more.

Bread Bakers Guild (@breadbakersguild)

Since 1993, non-profit alliance the Bread Bakers Guild has been sharing knowledge and skills. Their members include professionals, farmers, educators, home bakers, and more. On Instagram, the Bread Bakers Guild features gorgeous photography, inspiration, and additional resources for bread-baking fans.

Podcasts

Stella Culinary School

Hosted by Chef Jacob Burton, this podcast has instructional episodes that break down professional techniques for home cooks and bakers. Experts from all over the food industry drop in frequently for interviews. This podcast isn't bread-exclusive, so if you want to just listen to episodes about bread, seek out episodes 18-22.

The Sourdough Podcast

Fascinated by sourdough? This podcast features conversations from all over the sourdough community. You'll learn the stories behind the bread and get great tips on how to make it at home.

The Modernist BreadCrumbs

A podcast with episodes from 2017-2018, this special series from the Heritage Radio Network gets into the details of bread-making. You'll learn about different grains, the cultural history and science of bread, techniques, and innovations.

THE "DIRTY DOZEN" AND "CLEAN 15"

Every year, the Environmental Working Group releases a list of the produce with the most pesticide residue (Dirty Dozen) and a list of the ones with the least **chance of having residue (Clean 15). It's based on analysis from the U.S.** Department of Agriculture Pesticide Data Program report.

The Environmental Working Group found that 70% of the 48 types of produce tested had residues of at least one type of pesticide. In total there were 178 different pesticides and pesticide breakdown products. This residue can stay on veggies and fruit even after they are washed and peeled. All pesticides are toxic to humans and consuming them can cause damage to the nervous system, reproductive system, cancer, a weakened immune system, and more. Women who are pregnant can expose their unborn children to toxins through their diet, and continued exposure to pesticides can affect their development.

This info can help you choose the best fruits and veggies, as well as which ones you should always try to buy organic.

The Dirty Dozen	*The Clean 15*
• Strawberries	• Sweet corn
• Spinach	• Avocados
• Nectarines	• Pineapples
• Apples	• Cabbage
• Peaches	• Onions
• Celery	• Frozen sweet peas
• Grapes	• Papayas
• Pears	• Asparagus
• Cherries	• Mangoes

- Tomatoes
- Sweet bell peppers
- Potatoes
- Eggplant
- Honeydew
- Kiwi
- Cantaloupe
- Cauliflower
- Grapefruit

MEASUREMENT CONVERSION TABLES

VOLUME EQUIVALENTS (DRY) WEIGHT EQUIVALENTS

US Standard	Metric (Approx.)	US Standard	Metric (Approx.)
¼ teaspoon	1 ml	½ ounce	15 g
½ teaspoon	2 ml	1 ounce	30 g
1 teaspoon	5 ml	2 ounces	60 g
1 tablespoon	15 ml	4 ounces	115 g
¼ cup	59 ml	8 ounces	225 g
½ cup	118 ml	12 ounces	340 g
1 cup	235 ml	16 oz or 1 lb	455 g

VOLUME EQUIVALENTS (LIQUID) OVEN TEMPERATURES

US Standard	US Standard (ounces)	Metric (Approx.)	Fahrenheit (F)	Cels (C) (A
2 tablespoons	1 fl oz	30 ml	250°F	120
¼ cup	2 fl oz	60 ml	300°F	150
½ cup	4 fl oz	120 ml	325°F	165
1 cup	8 fl oz	240 ml	350°F	180
1 ½ cups	12 fl oz	355 ml	375°F	190
2 cups or 1	16 fl oz	475 ml		

pint			400°F	200
4 cups or 1 quart	32 fl oz	1 L	425°F	220
1 gallon	128 fl oz	4 L	450°F	230